The Way Home

THE WAY HOME

Essays on the Outside West

James McVey

The University of Utah Press

Salt Lake City

The Defiance House Man colophon is a registered trademark
of the University of Utah Press. It is based upon a four-foot-tall,
Ancient Puebloan pictograph (late PIII) near Glen Canyon, Utah.

14 13 12 11 10   1 2 3 4 5

LIBRARY OF CONGRESS CATALOGING-IN-PUBLICATION DATA

McVey, James, 1958-
The way home : essays on the outside West / James McVey.
p. cm.
ISBN 978-1-60781-033-9 (pbk. : alk. paper)
1. McVey, James, 1958—Travel—West (U.S.)—Anecdotes.
2. West (U.S.)—Description and travel—Anecdotes. I. Title.
PS3613.C83W39 2010
917.8'0433—dc22
2010028596

Printed and bound by Sheridan Books, Inc., Ann Arbor, Michigan.

For my mother and father

who showed me most of the trails,
and always the way home

Contents

Preface

Maybe a good place to begin this story is at the end of a long pier in downtown Cleveland. On a day so windy the sky blows itself clean, a boy of seven looks north across Lake Erie into a vast expanse of sky and water stretching clear to the horizon. The effect is instantaneous. For the first time in his young life, he beholds a world without so much as a sign of human presence. Born in the fifties, a decade many regard as the threshold moment in man's historic quest to control nature, he comes of age in a changing landscape—wetlands filled for shopping malls, woodlands cleared for subdivisions, mountains strip-mined for coal. But standing on the pier that day, looking out across the whitecaps, all that freshwater air stirring in his blood and bones, he senses an immediate recognition. On some level he must feel that it is not only a big natural space he is looking into, but a lifetime of possibility as well. The sound of crashing waves ringing in his ears, a cool wind blowing off the Canadian Shield, it might also occur to him that he stands at the brink of some awareness—some quality of experience that might define who he is as he, in turn, would try to define it.

If this seems like a curious way to introduce a book on the American West, well, consider it a confession of sorts—a roundabout way of admitting that I probably don't think of myself as a westerner, at least not in the classic sense, even if I have lived here a good deal of my life. The boy standing on the pier that day was me, of course, or at least a glimpse of myself as I might have been years ago. And while I am not native to the West, I often think of this moment as my first western experience. A sense of place can be a complicated matter, defined at various times by any number of factors. My affinity for the West would come naturally, as it turns out, and it would be firmly rooted in the land. Which leads me to this next point. If the West seems at times to be as much a state of mind as a place on the map, one thing ought to be clear: western landscape remains every bit as big and strange and wonderful as the wildest imagination.

This is a story of coming into a place with the idea, ultimately, of making it a home. The essays in this book all describe some form of nature or wilderness experience in the mountain West. All involve what Aldo Leopold called "primitive arts of wilderness travel." The hiking and river running and backcountry skiing function as ritualized activity, the purpose of which is to engage the elements of nature as a way of making a connection to place and feeling at home in the world. That all sounds fine, but it begins to get tricky once you get down to the particulars of what that means exactly. And that's what these essays explore. The particulars.

When I first arrived in Colorado more than twenty years ago, I knew enough to get into the backcountry, exploring some of the more remote and beautiful places of the West just to see what was there. I didn't reflect much on what I was doing or why, though it was clear from the outset I was drawn to these places. The West seemed to hold a kind of promise, and nowhere was this more evident than in its wild and natural areas. Over time, my reasons for being in the backcountry began to change, having less to do with seeing new terrain and more to do with understanding where I was. I found myself returning to many of the same places, something I rarely did in the early years. I read books on natural history and human history and anything else that might deepen my appreciation of where I was. While my interest in the West had taken on a different meaning, it all seemed part of the same project of exploration and discovery.

Eventually, I came to realize that if I were to consider any connection there might be to a wider world, I had to understand not only where I was but what I was doing there. Accordingly, the "primitive arts of wilderness travel" assumed a new significance. Whereas before they might have simply provided the means to get into the backcountry, they now became important in and of themselves, for they allowed for a certain kind of experience—a way of knowing based on sensory participation with the more-than-human world. It mattered how I ran a rapid or rolled a cast or what line I took through the trees down a mountain. The better I got at these things, the more intimately I could engage the natural features of a landscape. At some point it occurred to me that these were rites of initiation, all part of a long process of coming into a country.

It was also at this time that I began to think seriously about what it means to feel at home in the world. I had moved around a lot before coming to Colorado, living in six states in as many years and spending significant time in a few others. I was ready to settle down, feel grounded. For point of reference I thought back to my earliest memories of childhood, growing up in the hills and valleys of northeast Ohio along the glacial edge of the Allegheny Plateau. Memories of chasing fireflies on warm summer evenings. Slogging through crick muck for crawfish and tadpoles. Fishing for bluegill and catfish in neighborhood ponds, where mallards nested in cattails and painted turtles sunned themselves along the water's edge. This was the original imprint, where my sense of belonging in the natural world began. Any feeling of home I might find in the West would take root in similar fashion, that is, with an intimate connection to a local place.

And I found that place in the narrow ecotone of plains and mountains along the Front Range. From there, my sense of home would expand west to include the South Platte watershed, the Central Rockies, and eventually the canyon country of southern Utah. The horizon would move northward as well, though to less familiar terrain, to include the big wilderness areas of Idaho and Montana. Never a simple equation, my notion of home place would fall roughly in line with the Rocky Mountain chain. This was home ground, I believed, the place where I could take some measure of myself and view the wider world.

If my sense of place expanded over the years, so too did my sense of time. Drifting through the canyons of western rivers, I could trace a record of earth's history etched in the rock walls. Count the various times, for instance, an ancient sea covered the area. And just as the landscape looked different eons ago, it was sure to transform itself again in the future. This much was certain. But there was another reason now to look through the lens of geologic time. The planet was changing. Mass extinction and global warming, two phenomena that seemed virtually inconceivable a half century ago, were facts of life. Man's impact on the planet had become so profound as to convince some earth scientists that we've already entered a new geologic epoch. This was not the same world that existed for the boy who stood at the end of a pier so many years before. The environmental changes I witnessed then seem modest in comparison, more like a harbinger of bigger changes to come.

What I've described here, and what the essays allude to, is a long personal journey years in the making—a journey that traces its path by qualities of lifestyle and worldview. To the extent that a good deal of any story resides in the listener, the hope is that the reader will find something familiar and worthwhile in these pages. Time in the backcountry serves a restorative or salvific purpose, for sure, but I believe it goes beyond the personal realm, just as I believe the pursuit of Leopold's primitive arts amounts to more than aesthetics. If this story begins as a personal quest, its themes broaden as the focus shifts to the places themselves. And if this preoccupation with the backcountry has led to a lifetime of questions and concerns, it culminates finally in a conservation ethic.

This is a story of coming into a country, but it's also a story of coming into a life. A long journey home.

Acknowledgments

There are many people to thank for their support and friendship over the years, including those with whom I shared these and other adventures: Alan Adelman, Bob Baldwin, Joel Daehnke, Jeff Richards, Gary and Linda Vehrenkamp, Mo Wells. Thanks also to Tim Hogan, Lee Krauth, Blair Oliver, Armando Parés, and Annette Wenda for their assistance. Additional thanks to Ann Armstrong, Tad Pfeffer, and Bruce Rosenlund for sharing their time and expertise. Any misrepresentation of fact is my responsibility alone. I am especially grateful to Gary Holthaus and Peter Michelson for their enduring patience and encouragement. A writer could not have two finer mentors. Along the same lines, I would like to pay tribute to the memory of Edward Dorn. Closer to home, thank you Rosemarie and Kyle for being there and making it all worthwhile. As always, I am deeply indebted to my family, especially my sister, Laura, and brothers, John and Douglas. A special thanks to you, Edward Dorsch.

Without these people, this story would not be what it is. To you all, my deepest gratitude and heartfelt thanks.

1. *Life on the Edge*

Ecologists like to talk in terms of ecotones and edge effect when describing the border between two distinct ecosystems or bioregions. These ecotones can be interesting places, often supporting diverse communities of plant and animal life. For example, estuaries—those rich transitional zones where ocean meets continent—are among the most productive ecosystems on the planet. As you might expect, life on the edge can get exciting. Komodo dragons, for instance, like to hide in the forest cover along the edge of savannas where they use their quick reflexes to ambush unwitting prey—humans included—strolling by in the open. Recently, the edge effect has taken on a different meaning. With more and more clear-cutting of temperate forests, the added edge has made it easier for predators to raid the eggs and young of ground-nesting birds, and allowed parasitic species greater access to the nests of songbirds. These days, increased edge in places like tropical rain forests is usually synonymous with wide-scale fragmentation of natural ecosystems, raising the specter of species extinction and biodiversity loss.

For the better part of two decades, I have lived along a mesa in Colorado where the Great Plains meet the foothills of the Rocky Mountains. In this narrow ecotone between grassland and forest, the plants and animals of both ecosystems overlap to form a rich and dynamic community. The convergence of these life zones is magnified by the fact that this is where the Continental Divide reaches its easternmost approach in North America. This too is where the distance between the high peaks and plains is shortest and the gradient steepest. The landscape here is punctuated by the Flatirons, a dramatic sandstone formation that rises nearly three thousand feet from the Boulder valley floor. Along this edge of mountain and plain, a small community of cabins known as Chautauqua Park remains pretty much as it has for the past century. One of the last surviving sites of a cultural movement that began long ago in the East, Chautauqua enjoys its own edge character between grassland and forest, nature and culture, town and the mountains.

The Chautauqua movement was conceived in the late nineteenth century to provide educational programs for citizens who found themselves isolated from the cultural advances taking place in big cities. The Boulder site got its start in 1898 when a deal was struck with University of Texas officials interested in establishing a summer-school program. Boulder agreed to a rail line and offered seventy-five acres of an old apple orchard above Bluebell Creek. An auditorium and dining hall were built, followed eventually by cabins. Today, the Colorado site is one of only three permanently operating Chautauquas left in the country and the only site west of the Mississippi. Until recently, Chautauqua offered affordable nine-month leases to University of Colorado faculty and graduate students for the academic year. This arrangement worked out fine for those who didn't have many encumbrances, who didn't seem to mind the inconvenience of moving out for the summer, and who kind of liked the idea of having raptors and predators as neighbors.

I first arrived in 1986, having left my life east of the ninety-eighth meridian for a part-time teaching assignment at the university and a rough, untutored notion to write stories. To my way of thinking, the Rocky Mountain West afforded both the geographic and the psychic *space* to nurture this habit. In Colorado, I envisioned a life of writing and nature, adventure and wilderness. It's an old story, to be sure, with a late twentieth-century twist perhaps, but an old story just the same: pick up and move west for the promise of big spaces and new beginnings, freedom and opportunity.

But perpetual motion creates its own inertia, and it's the settling down, the staying put, that becomes difficult. From the ponderosa mesa above Bluebell Canyon, I could look across an ocean of treeless plains rolling to the eastern horizon—a visible reminder of the gulf separating me from all that I had been in my life. To the west, the Rocky Mountains reached into an open future like a vast geography of possibility. And there, poised between east and west, past and future, Chautauqua occupied the space in between. A good place to hole up and plan my next move, I figured, which is what I did until it dawned on me that while I had often wondered about my rootlessness—trying to understand it in the very process of taking steps to perpetuate it—it occurred to me that this *was* my home. At least as much as I could expect one to be. In fact, I came to like it here. It seemed to satisfy a desire to have it both ways. Step outside the cabin and I could walk to work at a major university; turn the other way and I was in the habitat of mountain lions and bears. This was my home, I decided, and I would take the time to get to know it.

A lone coyote howls in the warm night air, somewhere close by. His plaintive yowl draws me outside, past the last cabin and into the tallgrass meadow where I notice a movement of shadow along the forest edge. The coyote trots along at a casual pace, stopping from time to time as if distracted by something, all the while edging closer to the mesa rim that overlooks the city. I try to get closer, but he keeps his distance. When he moves, I can hear the rustle of dry September grass.

A faint reddish glow from the city lights reaches the top of the meadow, makes the coyote and his shadow barely visible. What is it, coyote, that has you so restless tonight? Without turning around, I know that the currents of warm air rising off the plains create a mirage of sparkling light. Is that it, coyote? All that glitter below, all those enticing city lights? Is that what you find so mesmerizing tonight down in the valley? Don't be taken in, brother. It's all glitter and no heart—all just fool's gold, coyote.

For the first couple years, I shared a small efficiency cabin with my friend and partner Rosemarie. Later, we moved to a larger one-bedroom with an empty lot next to it and an old apple tree that stood just outside the window. At our new place in cabin 506, we set up a desk where I sat down every morning to my new life as a writer. I worked in the early morning, usually, before walking the one mile down to campus where I both taught and attended classes. By late afternoon I was back at the cabin, ready for a hike in the mountains and what seemed like endless opportunities for backyard exploration along the miles of trails in and around the foothills and Flatirons. At some point I started to keep a journal, recording the various encounters with wildlife, interesting weather events, and day-to-day changes we could see taking place in the plants and trees around us.

We didn't plan it this way, exactly, but we found ourselves returning to cabin 506 year after year. There were other residents, graduate students mostly, who made the same migration back to Chautauqua every autumn. For those of us who got in the habit of returning, summer was a time to look for a temporary circumstance, usually in the mountains. All in all it was not a bad arrangement, especially knowing as you did that come September you had a place waiting for you down in town. Which is all just another way of saying that if autumn represents a season of departure and closure to some, to a few winter residents at Chautauqua, it signified a welcome return home.

These were good days, warm sunny days followed by soft moonlit nights: watching deer in the early evening under the apple tree next to the cabin, awakened at dawn to the *thud* of apples falling on the roof, an afternoon swim in one of the local creeks where flakes of mica flashed in the eddies like gold. And hikes. Hikes to Enchanted Mesa, Eldorado, Sunset Rock, Green Mountain, or up any one of the nearby canyons—Bluebell, Shadow, Bear, Skunk—to caves, waterfalls, arches, peaks. These daily hikes became a kind of ritual for me. For the next three months I could watch the trees and shrubs and grasses fade to autumn splendor, witness the long drama of bleeding chlorophyll and the slow bittersweet slide to winter torpor.

It begins in late August usually, depending on the weather and how much moisture remains in the ground: a touch of gold in the ash trees outside the cabin, a leaf of sumac gone red, a woolly bear in the grass outside…always something new to find, some new sign of the changing season.

In late afternoon, with the sun angling low for the ridge above Saddle Rock, Chautauqua Meadow shines like a tapestry of finely woven grasses. Flooded in golden sunlight, the meadow becomes a luminous fabric of threaded color so intricate as to nearly escape the naked eye. Big bluestem, faded to auburn, mixes with gray aster and sunflower. Little bluestem, a smaller finer grass, shows gold next to silver sage, crimson dock, wild rose. Of the lighter grasses, creamy Canada bluegrass and its cousin, Kentucky bluegrass, are the most conspicuous. Tough, wiry needle grass maintains its green beside timothy and drop seed. And the others: yucca, prickly pear, blue gramma (erstwhile king of the native short-grass prairie and an old bison favorite), side oats gramma, smooth brome, yarrow, the wheat grasses. Dispersed throughout the meadow, colorful stands of shrubs rise like islands on a tawny sea: yellow snowberry, red chokecherry, vermilion skunkbrush, copper ninebark.

At the western edge of the meadow a footpath weaves through a patch of ruby sumac before dropping down to a small creek, nearly dry now, at the mouth of Gregory Canyon. Gregory drains the north flank of Green Mountain and constitutes the first decent canyon north of the Flatirons. Here, broad-leaved cottonwoods grow beside green ash, willow, box elder, and wild plum. As the mixed meadow grasses merge with the dense riparian community along the creek, a ponderosa woodland begins along the sunny slope of the canyon. At various points all three of these communities converge in a mosaic of plants and trees.

The path follows the creek a ways before starting up the hillside, crossing broad slabs of exposed granite streaked with quartz. At 1.8 billion years old, this is some of the oldest rock found in the area. More than a century ago miners followed this trail with carts and pack animals, loaded with pickaxes and shovels, on their way to the gold fields of Black Hawk and Central City. Today, the only gold in sight belongs to dogbane, beaked hazelnut, and the riotous splashes of wild grape growing along the fluvial washes of the creek.

According to local botanists, low-elevation riparian forests along the Front Range—like the one here at Gregory—have plant-species diversity values as high as any reported in western North America. Higher on the trail, a new wave of flora corresponds to the change in elevation: Colorado blue spruce, Rocky Mountain juniper, mountain maple, and aspen. Higher still, a Douglas-fir community begins along the steep, north-facing canyon slope. Yet another vegetation type—composed of lichens and ferns and mosses— grows on the substrate of exposed cliffs, boulders, and talus.

To appreciate the full scope of diversity here, we need to include all the animals and birds and various species of flies, beetles, worms, mites, molds, bacteria…all the little guys who do the dirty work of recycling nutrients, converting atmospheric nitrogen to fertilizer, regulating the temperature and chemical composition of the air. And why stop there? It seems a bit arbitrary to separate these forms from the energy and nourishment they receive by way of their relation to light, air, water, soil, rock, organic matter. Indeed, the closer we look, the harder it becomes to distinguish one component of the ecosystem from the next.

Rather than considering life forms as separate entities, we might think of them instead as *patterns* in a matrix of interconnecting currents of matter, energy, and information. These currents establish interdependent relationships that bind each organism into a broader ecological web. Adapted to the conditions of their environment through natural selection, species evolve in concert with other species to exploit specific niches and serve particular functions. As the various species interact, they develop relationships that shape the environment itself. We impose concepts like "ecosystem" and "bioregion" to describe certain patterns in the biosphere that seem important to us. We do this for the sake of convenience, but, really, *all* of earth's species interact and participate in an interdependent, self-sustaining whole—a whole that encompasses the entire biodiversity of the planet.

I stop by the boarded-up lodge at the top of the canyon and help myself to the trickle of water springing from the well in back. The Greenman trail heads south here and continues up behind the Flatirons to the summit of Green Mountain. The trail is named in honor of a former Chautauqua president who was known for his habit of scattering apple and pear seeds along local springs. In fact, many of the nonnative species that inhabit the area owe their existence to early white settlers who brought reminders of their eastern heritage to local creek beds up and down the Front Range. I could follow Greenman trail to Saddle Rock ridge and a nice view of the Divide, but opt instead for the path less traveled—in this case, the narrow trail heading west into Long Canyon.

At the bottom of the canyon, a formidable clump of river birch grows along the creek bed. The birch trunks are thick, the bark smooth and bronze. This narrow draw supports an impressive array of plant life: waxflower, golden glow, horsetail, and star-shaped thimbleberry. I identify ninebark by its graceful leaves and tattered bark, as if recently scored by the sharp claws of a cat. Hence the name.

Most of the eastern woodland species found in the area were introduced by white settlers like Mr. Greenman. But not all. I continue up to the head of Long Canyon where at last I find what I'm looking for. *Betula papyrifera.* Thick, peeling clumps of paper birch. Hybridized with the local river birch, this is the only stand of *B. papyrifera* in Colorado. Black snakeroot also grows in Long Canyon. Agrimony, wild sarsaparilla, hazelnut, pin cherry, and wood lily, too. All of these species are associated with the eastern woodlands, but rather than being introduced like so many other species in the West, these paleoendemic plants are relics of the last great Ice Age. Today, they survive in a few ravines and gulches along the outer foothills—like windows into distant times and places.

More than a million years ago, the flora of the midwestern woodlands and prairies reached all the way to the base of the Colorado Rockies. Similarly, some of the Rocky Mountain flora—including pines and spruces—extended eastward to the prairies and woodlands. This interfingering of floras was disrupted during a period of post-Pleistocene warming. The extended drought and increased fire activity of this period ultimately produced the short-grass plains. As the eastern element shrank in areas west of the plains, some significant remnants were able to survive in protected mesic sites at the base of the mountains. Today, many species associated with the eastern woodlands and prairie continue to grow locally in wetlands, gulches, and north-facing ravines. Likewise, remnants of the Rocky Mountain flora (for example, limber pine) and some high-plains species (such as yucca and large-flowered beardtongue) can still be found as far east as the loess hills of western Iowa.

Took a stroll last night, following the loop around Enchanted Mesa to Bluebell Canyon. At the top of McClintock Trail, I paused to watch the bright light of Venus shining in the southern sky when, lo and behold, it slipped behind the mighty crag of the third Flatiron, disappearing from sight. A few steps back and the planet reappeared, only to set again behind the spire of rock. Another couple steps to the east and fair Venus, second planet from the sun, burst into view. With just these few steps I could trace the earth's rotation in space, feel the roll of stone at my feet.

From McClintock, the third Flatiron looked to be about one mile away. Venus, astronomers tell us, is anywhere between 25 and 160 million miles from

Earth, depending upon where each planet happens to be in its orbit around the sun. As an evening star, Venus is somewhere past superior conjunction tonight, though by how much is beyond me. The earth rotates on its axis at a mean linear velocity of 1,037 miles per hour at the equator. Here at forty degrees latitude, it's going to be less than that. Meanwhile, our planet's orbital velocity around the sun is in the neighborhood of 67,000 miles per hour. Venus circles the sun at an even faster rate of 78,000 mph. But nothing is fixed here, all is in motion. Our solar system spins in a galaxy that itself turns to even greater forces beyond. Thirty thousand light-years from the galactic center, our sun flies through the Milky Way at an average circular velocity of around 155 miles per second, while the Milky Way turns to the gravitational warp of superclusters far across the universe.

With the Flatirons looming close by, it doesn't take long to recognize what makes this place so dynamic. Here along the edge, everything invariably comes back to the mountains.

The Flatirons are part of a rock unit known as the Fountain Formation that runs the entire length of the Colorado Front Range and includes other such notable formations as Red Rocks and Garden of the Gods. The Fountain is composed of layers of sedimentary rock from an ancient mountain range known as the Ancestral Rockies. Formed three hundred million years ago, the Ancestral Rockies may have once stood as high as the Front Range before the forces of erosion washed them away. The deposits of sand, mud, and gravel eventually solidified to form the horizontal layers of sandstone, shale, and limestone that today characterize the Fountain Formation. Since then, at least nine other layers of sedimentary rock have formed on top of the Fountain, often corresponding to dramatic shifts in the earth's climate. In fact, an ancient sea covered this area for millions of years during the Cretaceous period. Today, fossils of fish scales and prismatic clamshells can be found in the exposed limestone shales of the Niobrara Formation, providing a glimpse of life as it was one hundred million years ago.

All these various layers of deposition would have remained buried underground, if it weren't for a major geologic upheaval that began seventy million years ago. Forces deep within the earth started a slow, irregular uplift that eventually produced the present-day Front Range and other parts of the

Rockies. As the Rockies uplifted, the overlaying beds of sedimentary rock fractured under the pressure, tilting upward along the edges of the uplift. This occurred along the eastern slope as well as the western slope. (The western counterpart of the tilted Fountain Formation can be seen today in such places as Maroon Bells.) This local uplift coincided with a broad regional uplift that eventually raised the plains to their present mile-high elevation. Meanwhile, the forces of erosion have been reshaping the mountain landscape, carving drainages into the upended layers of sedimentary rock.

As you might expect, this mountainous terrain plays havoc with the weather. The rugged topography of the Front Range disrupts the flow of large air masses across the continent, resulting in complex and often extreme climatic conditions. For much of the year, maritime air masses from the North Pacific bring cool, moist air to the Rockies, producing heavy snows. Air masses from the Gulf of Mexico back up against the eastern slope, creating upslope conditions and monsoon rains along the foothills. Summer convective storms occur almost daily, the result of hot air rising off the mountains. Some of these summer storms can be intense, producing hail and severe lightning, flash floods and tornadoes. High winds are common along the Front Range, especially during winter.

This maelstrom of wind and weather produces interesting atmospheric phenomena: wave clouds, crest clouds, inversions, undercast, and plenty more. It's not uncommon to find it snowing or raining without so much as a single cloud in the sky, or to see snow flurries and lightning and sunshine all at the same time. November is especially good for sunsets when long, polished streams of lenticular clouds hover over the foothills, reflecting the shifting tones of gold, crimson, and lilac.

In the dry rarefied air the heavens seem that much closer, the celestial spectacles that much brighter: lunar and solar eclipses, full solstice moons, planetary alignments, and the annual cycle of meteor showers—Perseid in August, Leonids in November, Gemenid in December, Eta Quarid in May. Like familiar landmarks close to home, the cycles and rhythms of stars help to locate us in space and time. We find the clockwork of the cosmos reassuring, even if we are reminded from time to time of our own precarious place in its great game of chance. Not long ago, we had the opportunity to view two major comets within the span of a couple years. For a few months in early spring, one could be sure to find Hale-Bopp fixed in the northern sky just after sunset, whirling through space at a speed of 98,000 mph, leaving a trail of ice and rock fifty million miles long. And if that weren't enough, a full lunar eclipse occurred one April night just about the time Hale-Bopp was at its brightest.

A coating of rime ice covers the ponderosas and shrubs in icy white spikes, like the grizzled whiskers of an old mountain man. The hoar grows thickest on the north sides of the bigger pines, but it seems to prefer the intricate lattice of shrubs best of all. Entire stands of skunkbrush—maroon now in winter—glimmer in a sheen of white crystals. Patches of apricot bluestem and matted bluegrass shine under the snowy glaze. A lone yucca stands apart, barbed with icy quills. Nature's familiar contrasts of dark and light are inverted, as the wet earth shows black against the white of frosted plants. At dusk, the surreal scene dissolves into a ghostly cover of ice fog that obscures all but the meadow and a few ponderosas at the edge of the mesa. By morning, this fantastic enchantment will all be gone, melted away with the rising sun.

By midwinter, most of the residents around Chautauqua are dug in pretty deep, observing age-old strategies to see them through the cold. Life goes on aboveground, of course, as evidenced by the fresh tracks of deer in snow, the print of a mountain lion embedded in ice. I keep a feeder in the apple tree outside the cabin, though I'm not sure who gets the better of the deal, the birds who feed or the birder who watches. From September to May, our avian neighbors drop in on a regular basis—wrens, finches, nuthatches, juncos, jays, flickers, woodpeckers, chickadees, tanagers. Magpies and ravens tend to stay away. Among the regular visitors, only the jays seem reluctant to honor the communal harmony. On one spring day all civility was shattered when a sharp-shinned hawk swooped down and picked off an unsuspecting sparrow, pinning it to the ground under its wings and talons.

For all its extreme weather, the foothills actually enjoy a fairly moderate climate. At forty degrees latitude and a mile above sea level, even winters are seasonable. Regular chinook winds blow off the Great Basin from the west, warming temperatures and melting snow. During these periodic thaws, Chautauqua's plants and animals spring to life. Tiny grasses and forbs sprout from the charred duff of recent burns. Willow branches turn florescent yellow with rising sap. With the snow gone, a network of vole tunnels becomes exposed in the meadow.

For human residents, too, winter is the time to begin thinking about spring. The price for living at Chautauqua—in fact, what makes it both accessible and affordable—comes up every June when renters are forced to vacate their cabins. For those returning in the fall, this means finding a place for summer that's big enough to store books and other personal items. For us, this translated usually into a small shack or cabin up one of the local canyons. This annual migration to the mountains became part of our regular routine—all part of the same cycle of seasons by which we patterned our lives. Many of these mountain dwellings were quite primitive and, in fact, rather forgettable. But there was one in particular that remains especially memorable.

A half hour's drive up Lefthand Canyon and another mile or so beyond the last crooked reach of road or power line, an old A-frame sits in a high alpine meadow on public land. To get there you have to park the car and hike a steep trail that eventually levels out on a plateau. No one seems altogether certain how the A-frame came to be; its sketchy history tends toward lore with each passing year. One story has it that weekend miners built the place fifty years ago when the price of gold became high. Another version tells how the A-frame was constructed by a group of Denver doctors who, for whatever reason, quickly abandoned the place. Somewhere along the way, somebody stopped paying taxes, and the A-frame managed to slip through the cracks of the legal bureaucratic grid. Field mice claimed it first, so the story goes, followed by a group of transients. Ultimately, it fell into the hands of a long line of fringe pilgrims who were willing to endure its many hardships for free rent and priceless solitude.

The system works like this. The current occupant is free to stay for as long as he or she chooses in whatever manner they see fit. When the occupant is ready to move, word circulates through the mountain community until somebody steps forward to seize the opportunity. A transition is arranged, and the new tenant moves in. Mountain etiquette generally stipulates that any and all improvements remain with the cabin.

And there have been many. Whoever first abandoned the A-frame left the place before finishing the job. As such, the cabin remains a work in progress, which is part of its appeal. When we arrived, the insulation and drywall on the inside had yet to be completed. The exterior finishing boards covered only a quarter of the outer plywood shell. The outside decking was only half done. The occupant of the A-frame reserves the right to work on any project of his or her choosing with the option, of course, to kick back and do nothing at all. As a kind of enticement, a good deal of the building materials that never made it onto the house remain *under* the house in the crawl space between the concrete footers, just waiting for some hack novice to come along and move them closer to where they belong. Which is what we did. It was all part of the fun, all part of the challenge.

It is not a major endeavor to live continuously without the basic amenities of running water, electricity, telephone, and so forth. Not as these things go. It's difficult work, to be sure, sometimes impossibly so, exacting a toll both physical and psychological. This is not about some back-to-nature panacea or survivalist utopia. Mountain living is hard, and it comes with its own set of problems: isolation, despair, loneliness, flatulent free-ranging cattle, gun-toting bozos. On the other hand, this *is* about lifestyle and choice— about taking stock and reducing needs, setting priorities and seeing to them, paying attention to the life around you and finding your place accordingly.

Most of my memories of the A-frame are good ones: watching snowfields along the Divide grow smaller in June with each passing day, seeing afternoon sunlight flash across the small creek down in the canyon, harvesting wild strawberries and raspberries, listening to nighthawks at dusk.

The meadow next to the A-frame was originally cleared to grow potatoes for local mining camps that appeared almost overnight in the 1860s: Rowena, Caribou, Gold Hill, Sunset, Wall Street, Salina, Eldora, Ward. Some are gone now, faded to ghost towns, or inhabited by reclusive mountain folk who seem to prefer it that way. At nine thousand feet above sea level, the meadow faces south and supports a wealth of wildflowers—penstemon, arnica, wild parsley, bluebells, lupine, paintbrush, asters, and more. During summer, the various blooms follow each other in waves of gold, blue, magenta, violet, scarlet. Sometimes, when the wind sweeps across the field, it looks as though the A-frame could be a wooden schooner tossed on a sea of rolling color.

In the next valley over, there's a turn-of-the-century log cabin that goes by the name of Glenclover. For a while we knew the family living there, and sometimes we'd make the hike across the meadow and down through the aspen grove to visit. On some of these occasions a few friends gathered to play bluegrass—traditional songs, mostly, with a few tunes of their own mixed in. They brewed their own beer, too, and sometimes we'd stay for hours, fooling around outside or just enjoying the high heavenly sound of stringed instruments in thin mountain air. I remember once late at night getting up to leave and closing the door behind me, pausing outside to listen to the faint melody that still played inside. Starlight washed the mountains in silver, as a bar of gold streamed through the cabin window from the oil lamp inside. I stayed a while, listening to the high trills of a mandolin drifting skyward for the stars—into a silence so pure it rang in my ears.

Started up the meadow today without any particular destination in mind, turning off finally at the steep gulch between the second and third Flatirons. The wind picks up out of the northwest, bringing the first clouds of a storm front spawned in the North Pacific—riding down along the jet stream that stayed north for most of the winter due to a particularly strong El Niño. The first snowflakes begin to fly even as sunlight still brightens the ponderosa needles. Not so fast, winter seems to say. On the way up I pass flowering spring beauties, grape holly, and pasqueflower. By morning, they'll all be buried under a foot of snow.

After a few hundred feet of elevation gain, I come across a large boulder outcrop tucked among the conifers. From its flat top I can see the dramatic pitch of the third etched against a graying sky, streaked in swaths of green lichen. I sit and watch a large raptor glide beside the Flatiron, tuck its wings and dive along the rock face. The outcrop is pocked with small depressions, filled now with snowmelt. Mud and pine needles cover the bottoms of these vernal pools. Looking closer I see tiny fairy shrimp, only a few millimeters in length, scooting through the water.

And how should tiny crustaceans find a home here, on the side of a mountain in the heart of a continent at the edge of the Great Divide? In fact, the American West is populated with a variety of shrimp species, some of which may be endemic to individual pools. The desert shrimp, cousin of the fairy shrimp, is more than three hundred million years old as a species. These Flatirons shrimp will hatch, mature, procreate, lay eggs, and die, all in a matter of a few days. Their eggs will lie dormant in the mud for a year or more until enough water collects in the pool to begin the life cycle again. Looking closer, I see the fairy shrimp are not alone in this particular pool. Scores of small aquatic worms, orange colored with black bands, squirm along the bottom. The snow flies faster, thicker. I gather myself and get ready to leave. Fish in the rocks, flowers in the snow . . .

With so much encroachment on natural habitats, it's inevitable that some wildlife is going to find itself caught in strange predicaments from time to time. Most of the encounters at Chautauqua are benign, even comical. I once encountered a dog owner on the Bluebell Trail, waiting patiently for his canine to return from a wild romp across the mesa with resident coyotes. "Happens all the time," he confided, twirling the leash. On another occasion I saw an eight-point buck trotting down Broadway, a major city thoroughfare, holding up rush-hour traffic before hanging a right onto Twentieth Street as if it knew exactly where to go for the most succulent crabapple patch in town—and it probably did. And then there are the dozen or so turkey vultures who roost in a tall willow in one of the more upscale neighborhoods in Boulder; the pair of coyotes over on Kohler Mesa who stay close to the den, lolling in the ponderosas, howling to the wail of sirens when the fire trucks pull out of Baseline Station down below; the mountain lions who filch toy poodles off the redwood decks of tony foothills homes, prompting calls from nature-loving property owners for a "safe" mountain environment.

One evening in late November, I was alerted to a loud rattle in the trash can out back. At the time, the cans were hung from the sides of the cabins to deter bears from raiding the garbage. From the screen door I watched a raccoon push back the lid, climb out of the can, drop to the ground, and waddle away. Apparently, it had climbed the handrail along the back steps of the cabin, where it then jumped to the can and managed to wedge itself under the lid. Piecing this together, I watched as a second coon pulled itself to the rim and dropped over the edge, scurrying off in the same direction as the first. More noise. By now the lid had slid far enough to the side to allow the third and last raccoon to emerge from the can, gripping a sizable drumstick in its paw from the Thanksgiving turkey we ate the day before.

Crafty critters.

But of all my experiences with wildlife at Chautauqua, none compares to the saga of Bear #9—one of Boulder's most celebrated citizens in recent memory. My first encounter with Bear #9 occurred at night while walking home from town. As I usually do, I crossed through the empty lot beside our cabin where the bird feeder hangs from an apple tree. On the far side of the dark alley I noticed a large animal rooting through the clematis beside the big cottonwood tree. Oh, I thought to myself approaching the back door, look at that big black poodle. Funny, I don't remember seeing a *poodle* around here before. The big black poodle made its way through the bushes to the cottonwood, where it reached up with its front paws and climbed twenty feet or so up the tree. It was about this time too that the poodle ceased to be a poodle and ascended rapidly up the order of mammals to something bigger and stronger and a lot more dangerous. I thought better of the alley, entered the front door instead, then proceeded to the screen door in back where for the next hour I watched the 175-pound bear knock over each trash bin in the alley and systematically pick through the garbage with a precision and patience that, under the circumstances, was most impressive. I mean, he opened *every* container and package and abandoned them only after extracting the last available ounce of nutrition. And he did all this in the bright glare of police car headlights that followed him from cabin to cabin. Eventually, a handful of residents came out to watch, too. Undeterred by all this attention, #9 continued his methodical search, going from trash bin to trash bin, turning down the alley behind Wild Rose Lane after finishing with our street.

A yearling male, Bear #9 was already a local celebrity. Because of his gregarious nature, he had been live-trapped earlier in the year and relocated to the Chambers Lake area near Cameron Pass—about fifty miles away as the crow flies. Just two weeks later, #9 found his way back to Chautauqua where he resumed his sociable ways: napping in a residential neighborhood, crashing a family picnic, rousting a group of (illegal) campers at Bluebell Shelter, joining hikers and joggers along the trails. He was trapped and relocated again, this time to Walker Ranch, only a few miles west of the Flatirons. But Bear #9 preferred his familiar digs at Chautauqua, returning two days later.

The official report on Bear #9 focused on the easy access to garbage and other human sources of food. His "mistake," it seems, was associating people with food. And why shouldn't he? After all, we humans usurp an estimated 40 percent of the planet's total biological production. By scanning our garbage, he was only fulfilling the evolutionary imperatives of opportunity and economy. Based on his meticulous inspection of Aster Lane, he was doing a fine job of it, too. As a "friendly" bear, #9 had found a way to coexist with the diversity of life occupying his particular habitat, in fact, seemed only too willing to do so. And while we as evolved primates rarely think twice about imposing ourselves on other species, they, on the other hand, rarely enjoy the same luxury.

Bear #9 was relocated a third and final time in the spring of 1991 to a remote area west of Walsenburg. Within a few weeks, a local hog farmer reported seeing a black bear that was "threatening" his pigs. When finally he shot and killed the animal, wildlife officials concluded that Bear #9 was probably not interested in the man's pigs at all, but rather his garbage.

A spring storm dumps a foot and a half of heavy wet snow along the Front Range. Around midnight, I start up the Mesa Trail along Bluebell Gulch just to check on things. The trees sag under their new burden, the limbs arch low over the trail. A thick ceiling of overcast presses down from above.

It seems that I'm the first one out tonight in the storm. A smooth, trackless plane of snow stretches straight ahead, down a long corridor of overhanging trees. A snowball, aimed just right, frees a limb of its heavy load as the tree springs back into position. I continue down the long tunnel of trees when suddenly a burst of red flashes across the open patches of white. The sky flickers with the color of blood. It's lightning, I realize, red lightning. Muted strobes of electricity, illuminating the low incandescent sky that tonight, in this spring snowstorm, reflects the red glare of city streetlights.

Along the edge of the mesas, Oregon grape begins to blossom as early as February. These clusters of bright yellow buds make a colorful bouquet next to their green and red leaves and the delicate sprigs of silver sage. Green ash, growing along the mouth of Bluebell Canyon, sprouts bronze tassels. Spring beauties bloom in tiny lavender stars. There will be candy tuff before long, as each day brings its own sign of the coming season: a kettle of turkey vultures circling high over the Flatirons, a purple hue in the leafless shrubs, an outbreak of dandelions.

Along the foothills, wildflower blooms follow each other in a long, choreographed procession of leaf and flower. Easter daisies follow spring beauties, which are succeeded by golden banner, chiming bells, and sand lily. Wild plum is among the first to blossom in the thicket of Bluebell Canyon, followed by hawthorn and dogwood. Mountain ash grows beside soft-leafed asparagus, Virginia creeper, box elder, and hazelnut. Patches of smooth sumac and snowberry adorn the higher, drier slopes next to juniper and wild rose. Toward the end of April, a yellow-shafted flicker *rat-a-tat-tats* a hole in the wooden auditorium, boring a home that grows bigger with each passing day, as if to announce, *The revolution has begun!* and to remind us yet again that what goes around must indeed come around.

In the steep gulch between the second and third Flatirons, a footpath winds through a garden of sandstone blocks wedged against pine and fir—as if only recently these colossal boulders tumbled from their high purchase and careened down the mountain in a long, thunderous rumble, witnessed only by the great herds of bison grazing on the plains below. About halfway up, the trail braids through a small oasis of trees where a network of animal trails converges. The trail climbs higher to a saddle behind the first Flatiron as a narrow band of snowy peaks appears over the ridge. The Great Divide. Traversing the slope of Green Mountain, I come to a pinnacle that looks south onto the backside of the third. I climb to the top, situate myself in a slot of rock, take out the binoculars, and wait.

My assorted grunts and sighs, boot scuffs on sandstone, all have alerted a large raven who now glides in to investigate, circles the outcrop once, and flaps over to the saddle where he alights on a large boulder. Head held high, the bird hops to a pool of rainwater, betraying his innate awkwardness on land. Still, there's something noble and even endearing about this glossy black scavenger. Not the most graceful or majestic flyer, the raven possesses a certain guile nonetheless—like he knows something you don't, and whatever it is, it has something to do with a joke, which has something to do with your mortality. The raven bides his time, confident that in the end he'll get what he needs.

The bird flies off the saddle, working hard. His motion is stiff and mechanical when he passes by, close enough to hear his wing flaps like the rustle of satin. Clearly, he hasn't forgotten about me. His throaty chortle reverberates through this natural amphitheater created by the walls of rock and curved flank of Green Mountain. The echoes ring loud and clear, as he swoops down a final time to serve notice that anyone who dares enter HIS lair would do well to beware.

Caaaaaaaaaw!!!

A soft breeze cools the sweat on my forehead. For a moment, the place is quiet again—opportunity for others to announce themselves. A squirrel, perturbed by something in the trees, completes a long string of maledictions like the protracted clicks of a ratchet. A cañon wren sings from across the way. Its curving cadence slows, drops in pitch. A Townsend's solitaire flies over the trees, its dipping flight pattern emulating the song of the wren.

This is a good place to eavesdrop on wildlife. Only a half hour from the back door of the cabin, this perch feels far removed from the bustle of town. Though a change of wind brings the faint din of traffic and construction from below, this mountain truly belongs to the animals and birds. Even at the cabin, as far as it is from downtown, the city's low dynamo hum feels close by. It's here on the rock where I come for the necessary separation.

Sometimes in late afternoon, sunlight filters through the trees on the back ridge, throwing long luminous rays into this cove of still mountain air. Once, I watched a flock of wrens whirl in unison through these streams of sunlight, alighting finally in a tall fir to feast on its delicate bell-shaped cones in a frenzy of muffled shrills. What a racket! The natural acoustics here, the spires of red sandstone, the high forest and blue sky, all lend themselves to a certain beauty and grace.

Finally, a peregrine emerges from a small recess just below the summit of the third. The falcon leans from the ledge and accelerates through the air in a burst of wing beats. Focusing on the bird, I don't immediately see the second falcon until it joins the first in a brief and furious free fall. For the next few minutes the pair engages in an acrobatic display of high-speed dives and rolls, punctuated by mournful shrieks that echo off the rock.

In 1991, peregrines returned to the Flatirons after an absence of thirty-four years. In the decades following World War II, their populations were decimated by DDT to the point that they disappeared altogether east of the Mississippi River. They're fast, perhaps the fastest birds in North America, capable of speeds up to 200 mph, and it's difficult to keep a steady bead with the binoculars.

Still, I get a good look at the talons, slate-colored back, the sheath of wings when they dive.

On the last approach to Mallory Cave, the climbing gets a bit dicey when the fissures leading to the keyhole are all clogged with ice. Still, with a little care, the final ascent is easily managed. Situated high along the north wall of Bear Canyon, the cave is a fortuitous accident of geology—huge slabs of fractured bedrock wedged together just so.

From the mouth of the cave, an impressive view of the foothills and prairie unfolds. To the north, Haystack Mountain stands alone on the plains—a remnant mesa separated from the foothills by an ancient river channel before the waterway changed its course in favor of a more southerly flow. But look to the south and the view turns grim. In the foreground, the Department of Commerce has seen fit to expand its facility at the National Institute of Standards and Technology by paving another ten acres of prime grassland. Somewhere inside this monolith ticks one of the world's most accurate clocks. Farther south, the Rocky Flats Nuclear Weapons Plant dominates one of the most scenic mesas found anywhere along the Front Range. For years, the weapons facility produced plutonium triggers for our nation's arsenal of nuclear warheads. Beyond Rocky Flats, the skyline of Denver cowers beneath its customary cover of pollution. Somewhere down there, below the brown smog, Rocky Mountain Arsenal—formerly a chemical weapons manufacturing site operated by the U.S. Army—once claimed the most poisonous square mile on the face of the earth. With a quick sweep of the eye, then, one can behold all these points of interest. Add them together and the story gets bleak. It's as if the most we can expect from ourselves is to be on time for our own mutually arranged destruction.

Surely we can do better than this. For starters, I propose an alternative way of measuring time—if this be a necessary endeavor at all. In lieu of atoms and lasers, let us use the cycles of seasons and constellations to mark our passage here on planet Earth. Why not orient ourselves to the regular visitation of meteors, say, or the seasonal rhythms of spring showers, summer monsoons, autumn

wildfires? Shall we place our trust in the march of evening shadows across a
meadow, or the time it takes for a planet to slip behind a mountain? Do we have
the foresight to gauge our progress by the gradual uplift of a continent? The wis-
dom to measure our deeds by the reflection of starlight on a field of snow?

By late May, the outer foothills near Chautauqua are vivid with blossoming
larkspur, pasqueflower, blue-eyed Mary, and yellow violet. These are followed
by waves of daisies, arnica, penstemon, lupine, cinquefoil, wild iris. Still another bloom sweeps the meadows and mesas by June: sulphur flower, harebell,
low sunflower, primrose.

Afternoons find me in the meadow, journal and field guide in hand, exam-
ining pistils and leaves. Counting petals and stamens. It's all I can do to keep
up with the carousel of blooms, the flurry of unfolding flowers. My efforts to
identify the various species seem obsessive at times, making me wonder what
it is exactly I'm after. All this note taking and classification strikes me as a bit
fastidious, yet I can hardly help myself. It seems I'm caught up in a spirit of
discovery. Within all this diversity of plant life lies a universe to be explored,
an infinite variety of form and strategy. Underlying my fascination, of course,
is the question of my own place. My relation to all of this. With so much
change and motion, I wonder what changes are in store for me. What new
incarnation? If there is something here to be learned about my life, its transience and transformations, I must pay attention. Take notice.

Meanwhile, butterflies cruise the meadow: mourning cloak, tiger swal-
lowtail, Weidermeyer's admiral, ocher ringlet, spring azure, checkered white.
(It's hard to say where all this winged color first originated, sunlight or wildflower.) Broad-tailed hummingbirds whir overhead, as everywhere Nature cel-
ebrates her bounty in an outlandish display of color and song and fragrance.
And it's not just the plants and birds and butterflies. A host of amphibians
and reptiles and mammals are busy too, on the move: tiger salamanders, lizards, mule deer, red foxes, porcupines, squirrels, prairie dogs, and meadow
jumping mice.

Fabric is the metaphor often used to describe the complex interdepen-
dency of species in an ecosystem. As various life forms interact and coevolve,
they weave relationships that contribute to an overall system of checks and
balances. This complexity of relations is what ensures an ecosystem's viability.

As with any resilient fabric, the integrity of an ecosystem depends upon a balanced tension, a consistency of texture strengthened by the binding mechanisms of all its strands. And as any good weaver will tell you, it takes time and patience for the pattern to develop. In the case of the North American grassland prairies, it's taken thirty million years for this ecosystem to evolve into what it is today. Eliminate a strand here, remove a thread there, and the fabric probably still holds together. But keep it up long enough, and eventually the whole thing begins to unravel.

In many cases, the health and productivity of an ecosystem depend upon a rich diversity of plant and animal life. In its broadest sense, *biodiversity* refers not only to the abundance of organisms and habitats on earth, but to the entire variety of genetic material as well. One of the most remarkable features of life on earth is its incredible diversity and complexity. The biosphere (all organisms combined) is confined to a relatively small area—a one-kilometer layer of soil and water and air extending over the outer edge of the earth's surface. From this thin layer, life has radiated into millions of different species. Ecologists believe that between 5 and 30 million species currently exist in the world, only a fraction of which (about 1.9 million) have been identified so far.

Although estimates vary, the rate of species extinction today is thought to be anywhere from one hundred to a thousand times higher than the rate that existed before the arrival of humans. Others put the figure closer to one thousand to eleven thousand times the natural or "background" rate. Not only are we losing species, but we are losing an incredible wealth of genetic information as well. Scientists estimate that if current trends continue, half of all species on earth could go extinct this century. Man has already caused the extinction of between 10 and 20 percent of the world's species. This rate rivals the rates that occurred during the five previous episodes of mass extinction, the most recent occurring sixty-five million years ago. In each of these episodes, it took ten million years of natural evolution to restore the planet's biodiversity.

Walking through Chautauqua Meadow among the wildflowers, in the midst of all this beauty and life, it's hard to grasp the full scope of what this all means. I can run the numbers in my head easily enough, but this hardly seems to get to the point. There's more to the equation that needs to be considered, a divide that needs to be crossed. At what point, I wonder, does all this loss begin to register in the heart? At what point does extinction become personal? Paul Shepard writes, "Animals and plants are correlates of our inmost selves in a literal as well as metaphoric sense—literal in the identity of their DNA and our capacity to analogize them as a society." Walking through the wildflowers, I understand the broader context: we live in an age of mass extinction. This is part of our world. At some point, the loss becomes our own. On some level, our destiny on this planet is linked to the destiny of all life.

Chinook winds roar through the night, hammering the foothills. The cabin creaks in the bigger gusts, gusts of 100 mph and better. The windows flex, the trees outside bend and groan. Around midnight, a particularly ferocious blast tweaks the small cabin just enough to bow the door frame and free the lock. The bolt unhitches and the wind blows the door wide open, pouring in pretty-as-you-please, rousting me awake just in time to see the rough draft of a novel (the story of my life), all 250 pages of it, rise off the plywood desk and spiral through the air in a long helix. Yep, I think, watching the blizzard of papers as the wind blasts off the Divide into our living room . . . yep, that just about sums it up.

On a sunny afternoon in late spring I start up the mountain through harebells and thistle, horsemint and paintbrush. Butterflies flash in the meadow like glints of sunlight on water: common sulphurs, swallowtails, cabbage whites, fritillaries. I lug a chisel and hammer, crude implements by today's standards, but tools that ought to do the trick just the same. In this case, it's the gesture that counts. There's a fresh pine stump above Bluebell Gulch that needs my attention. Or so I imagine.

Along the lower meadow, bluestem thrives in last year's burn area. Chokecherries fatten. A six-spotted tiger beetle confronts me on the trail, gram for gram perhaps the toughest carnivorous arthropod in all the territory. Black-eyed Susans soon will flower. Geraniums, too. The grasses will fade to gold and brown. A leaf of sumac will go red, and the whole cycle will begin again.

I bend down and scoop a handful of soil from the trail. Ecologists tell us that there's more complexity and organization in this little bit of dirt than on the surfaces of all the other planets combined. Thousands of species of bacteria alone. More information here in this thin layer of earth's biosphere than in all the known universe. This is the wonder, it seems to me. This cornucopia. This insistence of life to realize itself again and again—to fill the niches, adapt and evolve, to do what it takes to survive. To exist. Do we even have the language for such magnificence? Are we capable of the imagination or intellectual wherewithal or moral courage, not only to see but to believe?

I'm heading up the trail today to carve the head of a lion in a fresh stump of wood above Bluebell Gulch. I've located another stump over on Kohler Mesa that might be right for a grizzly or bison, eagle or wolf. Carving these modest totems, I pay homage to my neighbors the animals—those who live here, or once did. In the process, I honor my own place along the edge. It's all part of an overall project to bear witness, record, and remember. Keep track. All part of an effort to make this life matter.

2. *Privately Idaho*

During the summer we lived at the A-frame, Rosemarie and I were visited by a number of friends and acquaintances who came to see us out of curiosity, I suspect, more than anything else. Some, including a few of my colleagues at the university, seemed to eye our choice in lifestyle with a degree of skepticism, though their gifts of ice and beer were appreciated all the same. If nothing else, they came to the mountains to escape the brutal heat that gripped most of the West that summer. It was 1988, a year that will long be remembered for its hot weather and wildfires.

Among the visitors was an old friend of mine from back east, Bob Baldwin. Like myself, Bob had a passion for getting out and seeing new places. Since we both had some time at the end of summer, we sat down to plan a trip. We were trying to decide on a destination when Bob picked up the atlas at the North America page, turned it upside down, held it out at arm's length, and pointed to the big, empty white space near the bottom of the page. "There," he said, looking closer. "Mosquito Lake in the Yukon. That's where we'll go. Somebody just named it that to ward off the fickle. And look, not a road around for two...*three* hundred miles."

He had a point. We both wanted something particular from this trip. It didn't matter where we went so much as how. Bob and I had tried this sort of thing before. We didn't always follow a plan when we traveled, but it seemed we were guided by a few basic principles. First, as a matter of necessity, the trip couldn't cost much. It was also important that we went about it in our own way. In other words, no guides. Finally, as much as we could, we wanted to experience a place on its own terms. This could entail any number of things, since there may be many ways of coming to know a place. At the very least, we knew we had to minimize our intrusion. Since it was the backcountry where we wanted to be, this meant travel light. No machines.

After a bit of wrangling, we settled on the biggest, best-looking blank spot on the U.S. map. Central Idaho.

When we got up there, it looked like river travel might be the way to go—the best way to see the wilderness. In Stanley, we encountered the commercial shop and the dreaded package deal. Package included everything: guides, transportation, food, drink, equipment, entertainment, you name it.

It's not easy finding your own private Idaho, not even in Idaho.

On our way to the door, the guide stopped us. Perhaps he sensed our disillusionment. Maybe he knew the boredom and creeping despair of running group after commercial group through the same rigmarole all summer long. Maybe he too felt the yearning.

"Go north," he grinned. "There's a feller in Salmon who can outfit you. He's the last of the independents."

And so we did. We found John Blackadar at the back of his shop, surrounded by empty beer cans and piles of river gear. We told him we'd like to run the Middle Fork.

"Boated whitewater before?" he asked.

With some effort, I recalled a riffle on a certain stream of my youth. But this did little to settle my nerves. I knew we should ask a few questions, if for no other reason than to buy a little time. Like, uh, how best to run this river.

"Always stay scared."

Okay, fair enough. But what about this monstrous standing wave I see in this river guide?

"What about it?"

It looks dangerous.

"It is."

But... but what if we *flip the raft*?

"Don't."

He dragged out the gear: ash box, firebox with grill, five-gallon water jug, groover and seat, repair kit, cooler, dry bags, harness rig, a fistful of straps, foot pump, frame, seat, and one deflated fourteen-foot hypalon raft. When we were done, Bob noticed the half-dozen chaise longues leaning against the wall.

"River booty," explained our outfitter, grabbing two.

DAY 1

When we take off from Salmon, we aren't certain we can even land at our destination. The airstrip at Indian Creek has been closed for ten days due to a fiftyt-housand-acre fire in the backcountry. Land at your own risk, the policy seems to be. We fly west from town, and though it is still dark, we can see the brown folds of topography below. From the air, the canyons and gulches seem to be flooded with fog, but the smell of smoke at a few thousand feet quickly dispels the notion. The mountains become more rugged as we approach Indian Creek. To the northwest looms the solitary peak of Big Baldy, rose-tinted in the indigo heavens.

Upon our approach, the pilot looks long and hard after observing the cautionary red X at the end of the dirt runway. We circle once in the broad canyon, descending gradually. By the second go-around we aren't seventy feet from the tops of the trees. It's a peculiar feeling to be roller-coasting your way in a tiny twin-prop over the top of a dark and smoky mountainside, so close you can pick out individual boulders in the predawn light.

At last, we are safely down. The gear is deposited. A faint light blossoms in the east when the plane lifts again and disappears into the smoke.

Bob and I pack the gear and assemble the raft in the cold. As I pump life into the boat, we see twenty women and men in smoke-stained slickers carrying axes and picks, walking up from their riverside camp to the open tent at the ranger station. At the tent, they pick up radios and extinguishers. There are generators to carry, too. Some of the firefighters still have char on their faces. A helicopter rises from the runway to fly a group out to the fire.

The presence of firefighters at Indian Creek makes us conscious of our own reasons for being here. While their purpose is clear, ours is not so easy to define. True, we want to see this wilderness and experience it as fully as we can in the limited time that we're here. But what that means, exactly, may ultimately elude our understanding.

I have always felt that wild nature at its heart is trustworthy, a source of solace and wisdom. As products of the culture, we're bound to filter our experience in the backcountry through constructed models of understanding. And yet, as much of a paradox as it may seem, part of the reason for being here is to get beyond such prerogatives. We want to appreciate the place for what it is, be open to the influence of its beauty and wildness, remember and take with us all that we see and feel. This is where we place our trust: in the reality of what we find here.

By and by, the ranger shows up. We consult the map and decide upon four camps. He checks our gear for firebox, port-a-potty, et al.—the technology of minimum-impact camping. On the beach he goes over final details: pack everything out, catch and release with barbless hooks only, no soap within high-water marks. And with the firefighters waiting to be lifted out, we are ready to go.

We push off and gain the current. Immediately we are taken by the undulating landscape, sage-adorned and velvety brown. Solitary Douglas firs stand alone in the sun, casting stark shadows on the hillsides. We are deep inside the Frank Church–River of No Return Wilderness. Protected by the Central Idaho Wilderness Act of 1980, the wilderness represents the largest tract of undeveloped land in the Lower 48—nearly 2.4 million acres in all. Its mountains and canyons form the eroded relief of a 100 million-year-old granite underpinning known as the Idaho Batholith. Here, the irregular spines of the Sawtooths, White Clouds, Bighorn Crags, Salmons, and Bitterroots define the terrain. Volcanoes once frothed atop this 100-by-200-mile table of granite, succumbing finally to the wear of wind and rain.

The Middle Fork begins in the southern Salmon River range where Bear Valley Creek meets Marsh Creek. Fed by the likes of Dagger, Boundary, Sulphur, Lincoln, and Ramshorn creeks, the waters here begin an odyssey that will see them down to the Main Salmon, the Snake and Columbia, and finally out to the Pacific. It is an odyssey exceeded in magnificence only by the 2,000-mile journey *up*river by spawning salmon. Today, only a small fraction of these seagoing fish ever make it back to their Middle Fork birthplaces.

In higher water, river runners may begin at Boundary Creek (5,570 feet above sea level). We begin 25 miles downstream at Indian Creek (4,650 feet) and will reach the confluence at the Main Salmon some 71 miles later and 1,635 feet closer to sea level. The Middle Fork is 104 miles long, and running at 1,500 cubic feet per second in mid-August.

We float past three creeks before encountering our first class-III rapid where Marble Creek spills in from the west. But the whitewater here is mild and forgiving, and we handle it with ease. The river is low (2-foot average), so we must constantly look for the channel. More than once we have to get out to push off rocks.

Below Marble Creek we stop at Sunflower Flat to spend a few minutes beneath a cascading hot spring. The shower of water feels good in this high desert air. Years ago, this site was burned over when a camper lost control of his fire. The riverbank too shows signs of use and so we don't stay long, preferring instead the freedom of the moving current.

Down through Jackass Rapid, another class III, as we gain the homestretch to our first campsite. This is dry country, and the fragrance of pine is sharp in the air. We pass a hill that was burned over one or two years before. The whittled trunks stand straight and ash-white above a tawny ground cover that has since regenerated and dried out yet again. The brown hillside is splotched with crimson patches of late-summer snowberry.

We make camp on a wide sandbar across the river from Cameron Creek. A short walk up the hill reveals a pictograph panel under a small granite outcrop. One image depicts a man holding a bow and arrow, another the body and rack of a bighorn ram. These pictographs are believed to be eight hundred years old. Artifacts and pictographs found along the Middle Fork suggest that Native Americans inhabited this area for twelve thousand years. The Nez Perce and Shoshone roamed these parts until the beginning of the century when the last remaining band of Shoshone called the Sheepeaters, hiding out in the more remote parts of this wild country, vanished without a trace.

We make a modest fire and cook dinner. The river gurgles past as twilight blends to night.

DAY 2

In the morning we rise to a pair of eagles soaring over the river. A third bird—perhaps a vulture—approaches warily, keeping a distance. One of the eagles is heeled by a smaller bird. They drift to the south, where they disappear behind a ridge.

The wilderness is home to mountain lion, bighorn sheep, mountain goat, mule deer, coyote, bobcat, lynx, wolverine, elk, moose, black bear, otter, and more than a hundred species of birds, including bald and golden eagles, ospreys, red-tailed hawks, and wild turkeys. We can expect to find Dolly Varden, rocky mountain whitefish, white sturgeon, cutthroat and rainbow trout in the river. It will be another seven years before wolves are reintroduced here. Grizzlies, of course, remain absent. Without these two predators, this wilderness can never be truly wild. Still, it's reassuring to be among so much wildlife, including the quarter-ton sturgeons rumored to be lurking in the deep channels of the Main Salmon, even if they've been known on occasion to gum the leg of an unsuspecting swimmer.

Short day on the river today. Just twelve miles before we make our second camp at Loon Creek. On the sandbar we find a shady nook behind an alder thicket where the creek comes in. The raft is secured to a rock, and all the gear is up. We've been told of a hot spring only a mile up Loon Creek, but we're in no particular hurry.

I sit beside the creek and listen to the water pushing over stones, swirling around boulders, plunging through falls. I look at the sun-flecked rivulets, the eddies and pools. Just now, the world seems sacred. Mere conjecture, perhaps, but here beside the river it's enough just to wonder.

Eventually, we make the hike to the hot spring, where I leave Bob and continue up Loon Creek to fish. The trail is wide and easy. This is the route used by the cavalry more than a century ago during the Sheepeater War. "I've come 10 miles," cavalryman Barnard wrote, "from 10 foot snow to roses and rattlesnakes." I walk a mile above the hot spring and peer down the embankment to the terraced boulders and pools descending to the mouth of the canyon. It was here that a group of murdered Chinese miners was found. The year was 1879, and the Sheepeater Indians were blamed. Brig. Gen. O. O. Howard ordered troops to the Middle Fork—the same General Howard who with twelve hundred soldiers tracked Chief Joseph's band of seven hundred Nez Perce along their historic thirteen hundred-mile trek to Canada.

History remembers Chief Joseph as the brilliant military strategist who time and again outwitted the cavalry along this now legendary trek. But the Nez Perce didn't share the white man's zeal for centralized authority. The Nez Perce recognized the right of each warrior, of each individual, to act on his own. It seems more likely that the remarkable success in getting as far as they did was due to the skill and initiative of all the Nez Perce, not just Chief Joseph.

The Nez Perce traveled down the Salmon River canyon and across the Bitterroots to within fifty miles of the Canadian border. It was in the Montana Bear Paws where they finally decided that freedom away from their sacred lands—along the Columbia and Salmon and across the Montana plains—was not freedom enough. Perhaps two hundred escaped to Canada. But for most of the Nez Perce, the trek was over. They surrendered under the promise that they be returned to the Lapwai Reservation in western Idaho. But the promise was never honored. Chief Joseph and the last of the Nez Perce who didn't cross into Canada, those remaining of one of North America's greatest tribes who didn't buy into the white man's ways…those Nez Perce were banished to Fort Leavenworth and then later to the Indian Territory.

The Sheepeater War followed a similar script, if less heroic. The cavalry trudged more than twelve hundred miles through these mountains, often lost and cold and hungry. They rarely encountered the Indians. The story goes that the Sheepeaters seemed puzzled and finally bored by the pursuit of the army. Some surrendered and settled on the Fort Hall Reservation in eastern Idaho. Some missed the surrender ceremony altogether and remained in the mountains for many more years.

I cast into an exquisite pool, but something tells me to stop. It's not the place. Not the time. In this canyon everything is distinct, set perfectly in place. So much so that the reality of it seems overwhelming. For a moment there's no difference between now and a thousand years ago, between now and a thousand years *from* now.

I follow the river down to my rod case. Colossal boulders, worn smooth by the elements, buttress the creek. There are defiles and hidden passageways to slip through. Sometimes I have to climb over a boulder and scramble back down to the ground.

Later, Bob and I sit in the hot spring where starlight flashes off the bottom gravel, and shooting stars streak across the sky.

Day 3

Back on the river the Shoshone called Tom-Agit-Pah, or "big fish water," after the chinook salmon.

It was cold this morning at first light. Near freezing, one guesses, when shocked out of a pleasant slumber to move the toes, bury the fingers, cover the nose. It's nice to camp where the ridge is low in the southeast, but this is not always possible. Especially as we drop deeper into the canyon. When the sun finally spills over the rim, the change is dramatic. Temperatures will reach the upper eighties today, and dip below forty again at night.

As hot as the sun burns at noon, the river water is cold. Cold and clear as any I've seen. In the morning, its color blends from beige to aqua to deep green and black in the pools. By afternoon, when the sun reaches its zenith, the river becomes transparent. The water is so clear, not even sun shafts form. And later, when the sun slants hard by the ridge in the west, the river reflects the ocher and gold of canyon walls.

Past Hospital Bar and the last hot springs camp on the Middle Fork. On we go toward our class-IV initiation at Tappan Falls. We float by dry creek beds—Aparejo and Cub and Cow—that tell of springtime's raucous power. In these chutes of bleached rock we envision frothy water pushing limbs and logs, undercutting the bank, scouring the wash. We imagine boulders gnashing against one another.

Tappan I rapids deposit us in a long calm pool, just above the falls. The map tells us to scout, and we do. Standing on a rocky bank overlooking the falls, we plan our strategy.

"Enter just to the left of that widowmaker," Bob says, pointing to an exposed rock at the head of the falls. "Then watch for that devil's pitchfork, those two sharp rocks, down at the bottom."

By now we've fashioned our own vernacular to describe the various hazards and features of the river.

"And make sure ole purple [our essentials bag] is firmly lashed and the zipper tight," he smiles. "We'll want our money dry when we arrive at Cache Bar."

We push off and float toward the falls. Nerve-racking, this calm before the storm. A deep breath and here we go. We slip over the edge and drop ten feet into whitewater, watching for the two rocks downstream. I pull back on the oars just in time to skirt the hazard. It all happens in a heartbeat, before we're adrift again in the foamy water below.

Downstream, we tie up under the shade of a willow and enjoy a lunch of sardines, crackers, and figs. But we don't stay long, preferring the lulling pace of the river instead.

As the open country rolls by, it leaves an impression on the senses: The gentle slope of tawny hills graced by solitary firs. The fine, natural curvature of talus winding its way through sage and fir. Willow and alder lining the river, but never enough to clutter. Ledges and crevices. The high ridges hard against a cobalt sky—ridges that never seem too high or rugged to climb, hills never too steep. And the river, always the river. Now tumbling white and furious against waterscaped granite. Now roiling and shimmering in a distorted reflection like something from Monet. Now so still and clear that you could be floating on air.

When it gets too hot, we jump in and hoist ourselves back aboard the raft. In the slower water, a fly is slung for the eddies and pools. Always an eye on the ledges for a ram. We've seen plenty of ewes and their crisscrossing trails traversing the hills.

And down we go. Past sand bars, timbered benches, steep walls, and sagebrush flats. Past Camas Creek and all the camps: Johnnie Walker, Funston, Broken Oar, Sheep Creek…

Haystack Rapid begins a two hundred-yard pinball maneuver through rock gardens. We apprise ourselves of the map's directions. This works for about a half minute before we simply wing it, staying in the deep water to avoid rocks and the exasperating halt of heavy rubber. I try to scout a clean passage as Bob reefs hard on the long oars to get our cumbersome craft across the river into a different channel. It's hard work, but pride has entered into the picture. It's very satisfying to run the river correctly without bouncing off rocks or getting hung up, for it can be even harder work to spin and pivot off a rock.

Most of the time, our primary objective is to keep the raft in the main current while avoiding all rock in the form of walls and widowmakers. This seems simple enough, but the challenge is—provided that you've read the river correctly and that no "sleeper" lies in wait under a benign-looking "pillow," or that you can stay in the river's "tongue," or that there is a tongue at all—the challenge is to maneuver the raft into position through a particular rapid. If the river bends sharply in rough water, it's best to stay just to the inside of the tongue. Too far inside or outside, and the raft could wash onto rocks where you run the risk of flipping. Watch too where the river rushes under a wall. The power of whitewater should not be underestimated. It's best to pull back on the oars, as this affords the most control and time through a rapid. A little laziness, one small breach of concentration, and the river will beat you.

The rock garden is successfully negotiated. The sound of whitewater recedes upstream. Bob is exhausted, but exhilarated just the same. Navigating around the rocks has worn him out. This, of course, is part of the deal. We both know it, and slowly a grin creases his face. It's another five miles to our camp at Wilson Creek. The country is more rugged now. From here to the confluence we should expect steeper canyons, ledges, a rougher terrain overall.

We shoot Jack Creek Rapids, a class-III stretch cleaved in the center by a large earthquake rock. The map tells us of giant waves at high water, and again we're left with our imaginations to picture a raging Middle Fork.

At Wilson Creek the river pools up in a long, luxurious stretch of emerald. We drift a while before landing. Water droplets fall from the oars, making a sound on the water as light as the breeze blowing down the canyon. Our camp tonight is situated along a wide sandbar, crowned in the middle by a big ponderosa reaching eighty feet in the air.

The sand is hot to the step as we scurry for cool relief beneath the tree. We empty the raft of gear and quickly set up camp. Time for a beer and whimsical revelry. But something is amiss. Ah yes, the headgear. Hats are retrieved from the raft and positioned accordingly. But wait, there's something else. The chairs! To the boat again and back. The *chairs* are unfolded, and there we are: in the shade of a giant ponderosa on a beach soft as silk, watching curious cutthroat inch closer in the most beautiful river on earth.

Time to count blessings: family, friends, wild country. That done, we contemplate future adventures.

"The Serengeti, Denali, Talkeetnah," Bob declares. He wears an Australian bush hat with a chin strap, the brim snapped on one side. But it's much too small for his head, and it's hard to take him seriously.

"Belize and Bali," I counter. "The Bahamas and Borneo."

The sun slides behind the far ridge as a slight chill descends. Downriver, a sunny bench of sand beckons. We pick up our chairs and move down.

Back to the global reaches of our minds.

"Portugal and Paris."

"Down under to New Zealand."

"Florence and Venice."

"The Christmas Islands."

"Pago Pago."

Long, cool fingers of shadow eclipse our bench as we move once more, until it's clear that if we dare to bring this day back yet again, we'll have to climb.

And so we do, up a mild talus slope till we are high among the sage and fir, where gnarled shrubs grow improbably out of rock. Far below us, the Middle Fork snakes past the sandy flat of our camp. The river looks gentle from up here, like a lazy watercolor streak.

Across the canyon, the peaks and cliffs are bathed in luminous shadow, somewhere between day and night, as the sun takes its final bow. There's a kind of music in the mountains, better felt than actually heard. Listen well one evening, as twilight plays from ridge to ridge into an endless ocher of sky.

Day 4

One more night on the river that perpetually resists metaphor. Now four days of canyon walls and sage slopes, and slowly the senses modulate. Out here, history tends toward collapse, and the improbable seems likely. So it is with the world when the insular layers of convention and familiarity are peeled away.

A fond farewell to Wilson Bar as we catch up with the current. This morning we are escorted down a half-mile stretch of river by two curious otters. They surface and sound not an oar's length away. While we plow through the water, the otters move about at will. Drifting along, it becomes clear that *we* are the observed.

Just fifteen miles today to our last camp at Tumble Creek. We stop at Rattlesnake Creek Cave to view more Indian pictographs. The shallow cave bears testimony to the basic human urge to re-create the world. It seems appropriate that these images, painted with mineral oxides mixed in grease and water, are among the few artifacts that have survived through the centuries. The world filtered through the lens of human imagination.

The canyon deepens with every passing mile; the rapids become more severe. We run Waterfall Creek Rapids, a class III, careful to avoid the hazard in the center. Below the rapid, Big Creek Bridge looms hundreds of feet above the river, but the creek is dry and we see only the waterworn contours in the rock.

I have my fly fishing gear out this morning, taking advantage of the quiet stretches of idle water. We enter Cutthroat Cove, where I proceed to hook a nice twelve-inch trout. Upon its release, we watch the fish swim away through the sunlit turquoise of the pool.

A mile farther we float under Veil Falls, reduced now to a wisp of water streaking from a cliff two hundred feet above the river. The falls are impressive, if somewhat subdued in late summer. At peak levels in June, the Middle Fork will surge as high as thirteen feet. Half that height is regarded as extremely hazardous for river runners. We are satisfied in our two-foot stage, though another couple of feet would be nice, especially in the shallow sections. Make for fewer snags and scrapes.

A group of kayakers catches up with us. They are guides from McCall, scouting the Middle Fork in anticipation of leading raft trips here next summer. The kayaks dart and pivot, and I can't help notice how adroit they are in the water. There's more opportunity for personal control. On the other hand, a raft is more closely bound to the force and whim of the current, a fact that suits us well. As quickly as they arrive, the kayakers move downriver out of sight.

As the canyon narrows, the rapids appear with greater frequency. Redside Rapids, classified at its worst as IV, is as challenging as any we've encountered. A massive boulder splits a falls, and we opt for the right channel. There's a sharp turn we must execute in fast water, and we don't make it all the way.

The raft turns and grinds on a boulder, pushed sideways onto more rocks. Not good. We struggle to free the raft from the rocks, but the pressure from the rapids is too much. Finally, we both must get into the river to lift it off.

"Can't relax after running Redside Rapids successfully," the map confides, granting us a generous benefit of doubt. "Weber Rapids is as mean or worse." We enter the flow left of center and work to avoid the rocks. Only once are we thrust into a hole and forced to pull out.

Adrift in a froth of flat water below the rapids, we rest and judge our performance down Redside and Weber. But not for long. This canyon is too magnificent, the river too beautiful.

We float by camps bearing the names of past adventures, mishaps, and mysteries. Each is rich in its own peculiar lore: Papoose, Ship Island, Lightning Strike, Parrot Placer. Prospector Earl Parrot worked this latter stretch of river during the early part of the century. It seems Earl was unlucky in love and flat-out disillusioned with society. We conjure up our respective images of Earl and his exploits.

I'm reminded of another past denizen of the Middle Fork, perhaps the most notorious of them all: mule packer Dave Lewis. Cougar Dave, as he was later known, came with the soldiers during the Sheepeater War. A Civil War veteran who survived the siege at Vicksburg, he was a scout with Captain Benteen when they arrived at Little Big Horn just after the battle. Lewis hunted cougars in the Middle Fork country, killing more than six hundred, it is said.

Then there's Charlie Norton, the noted bear hunter in and around the Custer area who eventually got too close to a grizzly. The grizzly mangled Norton and crushed his face. When his friends found him, they extracted a quart of maggots from Charlie's wounds and removed all his shattered jaw. Charlie survived the ordeal but was burdened for the rest of his days with a mouth that kept growing shut, a mouth that had to continually be cut open. Without anesthetic. Despite it all, Norton went on prospecting. On one occasion, he had to cut his mouth with a pocket knife and hand mirror after his prospecting buddies refused to help. Finally he died of old age, bemoaning at the end that he was "getting to be a damned baby" for flinching at the thought of additional operations. The newspaper in Pocatello remembered Charlie as "essentially a man of nerve."

Center-left looks to be the most fun, so I cheat that way above Cliffside Rapids. The river drops and turns hard to the right at the runout, where standing waves bellow and roar. The river carries us toward the rock cliff. I pull back on the oars, but the power of all this tumbling water is too much. We bounce off the wall into the frothy swirl below.

Lower Cliffside Rapids is upon us, as we switch: I to the front, Bob to the helm. It's a rock-garden maze, and my scouting directions prove utterly worthless. "Do us proud," I say, because now the kayakers are watching from the holes and eddies below the rapids. We do our best....

The kayakers pivot and regroup downriver, afforded a demonstration of how *not* to run Lower Cliffside Rapids.

We make camp on a small bar by Tumble Creek—our last night on the Middle Fork. We cook a fast dinner, watching the wind breathe mystery into the embers of our fire. The sand glows pearl in starlight, while the canyon walls rise to where the ridge cuts black against indigo.

And always, the gentle murmur of water passing by.

Day 5

Eight miles to the confluence and another three below that to Cache Bar takeout. We putter around camp, brewing coffee, cooking eggs, stuffing sacks. The sun eclipses the canyon rim, washing us in warm light. We're a little hesitant this morning, anxious to get on the river, but reluctant to leave it too. Finally the bags are packed, the gear lashed tight. We unhitch and steer for the current.

A little ways down, we wave to the kayakers who are only now stirring in their camp. Will they get their permit to guide, I wonder. Will any lose their lives on the river like so many who have gone before? What destiny do they have? Do *I* have? And for a moment I'm startled by the unaffected candor of my questions. The rare sincerity.

The river will do that to you.

We may be finishing our journey today, but there's still Rubber Rapid to run, a tough class IV that won't let us forget there's still some of this river to negotiate yet, boys, and best you strap down and eye up. "This is the heaviest whitewater on the river," the map states flatly.

We're at it again, looking for rocks, nosing the bow into a tongue convoluted with standing waves…around widowmakers, through a pitchfork, and down over falls. Sheer whitewater fun.

There are more rapids to run. Hancock, Devil's Tooth, and House Rocks pack the most punch. But down here the river is hurrying toward the confluence with the Main Salmon; the individual rapids flatten out and merge. We pilot the raft through them anyway. The last few days we've paid the map less heed and counted more on our experience at reading the river. If there's no warning to scout, we run the rapid as is.

The canyon intensifies, the walls get steeper. It's all whitewater to the last reach before the confluence. Our river savvy has become automatic: seeing the tongue, deciphering the channel, reading pillows, sleepers, haystacks, and holes. All have become second nature. Stomach butterflies now as the flat water gets sucked over a falls, pulling the oars in during a squeeze between rocks, pivoting, turning, reeling…

And when it's done and the confluence unfolds at the end of the canyon, the water now flat, amassing toward yet a deeper canyon (calm, as if resigned to the inevitable union with the Main Salmon), the Middle Fork plays out.

Turn a lazy circle in the raft and take one final look upriver…

Love many, trust a few
Learn to paddle your own canoe

3. *A River Wild and Free*

In the canyon country of the desert Southwest, a number of rivers and their tributaries flow through the landscape like arteries coursing through the body, providing for a host of plants and animals along their narrow corridors. We know them by name: the Colorado, Green, Dolores, San Juan, Escalante, White. And their many canyons: Grand, Cataract, Desolation, Gray's, Still-water, Labyrinth, Slick Rock, the Goosenecks. And just as the water of all rivers must eventually flow together, our time in these remote canyons finds its way into the heart. It happens simply and quite naturally—in the play of sunlight on swirling water, the sound of rapids, the feel of quicksand between toes. Floating through the desert on a live current, the body tunes itself to the rhythms of the river.

The Yampa River begins along the eastern flank of the White River Plateau before flowing in a westerly direction onto the high desert of northwest Colorado and Dinosaur National Monument. Rosemarie and I have come to its whispering banks and sandstone canyons for all the usual reasons. We've come to take cover, forget so we might remember. We've come looking for the West, the natural *unimproved* West. And in our own particular way we've come to bear witness: to run this river's free-flowing waters and to find out what it means to float the last unimpounded major tributary in the Colorado River system.

The first thing we discover is that without regulated flows above, water levels on the river drop suddenly and dramatically. The Yampa is bony, running at eight hundred cubic feet per second, down 75 percent in the past week after sustaining itself at two thousand cfs for nearly a month. But there are advantages to this: the commercial trips are done for the year, the beaches are dry, the weather mostly stable. Better yet, we'll be the last ones to run the river this season with no one coming down behind us. This is not a big deal, usually, but this time we've forsaken the relative safety of a raft for a more versatile sixteen-foot canoe.

The next thing to recognize about this river is that it is not unimpounded at all. In fact, there are a handful of dams along the Yampa and its tributaries. But these are all small dams upriver, and none is big enough to significantly affect the Yampa's free-flowing character. Of course, this might have all been different once. Ever since Earl Douglass found eight *Brontosaurus* bones here in 1909, Dinosaur Monument has enjoyed the protections of the National Park system. In 1939, the monument was expanded to include the Yampa canyon and sixty miles of the Green River from Brown's Park down to Split Mountain. By the 1950s, however, the Bureau of Reclamation had proposed a major dam for Echo Park that would have inundated forty-four miles of the Yampa and another sixty-three miles of the Green. The forces of preservation rallied to the cause, as Dinosaur became the site of one of the most important conservation battles ever waged in American history. That battle was won. But conservation victories are temporary, their defeats permanent. Not long after the canyons of Dinosaur were saved, Glen Canyon was lost and with it one of the more beautiful landscapes in the West. To this day, there are at least two major dams still on the drawing board for the Yampa—dams that, if built, would forever change the "wild and free" character of this river.

The current sighs along the bank. Cloud shadows steal across the sage flats on the other side of the river. Dry bags are packed, ammo cans loaded. A final check of things before we lower the canoe into the muddy foam below.

We'll float the entire length of Dinosaur Monument from Deerlodge Park in the east to the mouth of Split Mountain in the southwest. The monument extends over 325 square miles along the eastern plateau of the Uinta Mountains. From the put-in at Deerlodge, it is 47 miles down to the confluence and another 26 miles on the Green—about 73 miles in all with a modest vertical drop of 815 feet. More important, it means four nights on the river. Not a lot by some standards, but enough to get the feel of it.

The river is flat and wide through Happy Hollow, down past Vale of Tears and Disappointment Draw. Fitting names for this land of extremes. Not a mile from the put-in we come upon a large golden eagle at the edge of the river, clutching a fish in its talons. An auspicious beginning, to be sure. It's not long, though, before I misread the channel and run the canoe up on the rocks, a gentle reminder of how low the river really is. All hands overboard now to get the craft back into the channel on the other side of the river.

"Who's guiding this vessel, anyway?" chides Rosemarie, mischief in her Irish eyes.

But it's a friendly banter. We both know how fortunate we are. It's the high desert out here, and this is inimitable Dinosaur.

From the open flats of Deerlodge, we enter the canyon through Yampa Portal along an impressive corridor of sandstone. Red and gray strata, sloping upstream, bear the familiar black stains of mineral oxidation. Higher up, the gold and buff walls appear undulated and weatherworn. Sage hills and juniper benches trace the irregular formations. As much as we're impressed with the spaces of the canyon, we know too that we are looking far into time. Over the past fifteen million years, the river has cut fifteen hundred feet and hundreds of millions of years into the uplifted rock, exposing sections of the earth as old as the Permian. The geology here reads like an ancient text: sand dunes, riverbeds, ocean floors…all frozen now in the uplifts and folds of the canyon walls. Add the finishing touches of frost and wind and rain erosion, and what one sees finally is an elegance born of antiquity.

The run down to Tepee Hole is just ten miles, but the low water makes it challenging. The afternoon sun transforms the river into a dazzling mosaic of silver and white light. Down we go past Anderson Hole, through a series of runs around Thanksgiving Gorge and Corral Springs Draw—watching for the channel, beginning now to unwind, to unravel the habits of perception acquired in town.

A beach, another bend, and Tepee Camp comes into view. We backpaddle into a broad eddy and make for shore. From the beach, we can hear the deep rumble of rapids echoing through the canyon below.

But that's tomorrow.

Right now it's time to unload the gear, set up camp, and head back to the river for a swim. There are still a few hours of daylight left, and the water temperature feels good. I venture in until the heat of the sun is offset by the cold of the river, right about *there*. Now to sit down. I find the place on the beach where the balance of temperatures is most comfortable. Across the river a canyon wall conveys the indifference of a million years, and I'm left to wonder how something so sensitive as the human body could ever find a home in this universe at all.

At dusk, we head downstream through a maze of pygmy juniper trees that look fairly enchanted in the twilight. A delicate crust of cryptogams covers the ground, and so we keep to the path, following it through the trees to an overlook above Tepee Rapid where we can scout the river.

Looking down, Rosemarie sees a way through the rapids. "Keep that first rock on the right," she says, "then head for the large hole at the bottom of the upper rapids, staying just to the right of it. After that, we can pick one of two passages—the one to the left has that hazard, but a fun little drop just the same."

Committing this to memory, we weave our way back through the trees to camp, dinner, and a fire. As darkness falls, we watch the sky. Venus slips behind the canyon rim in the west as the Corona Borealis appears overhead. Sometime in the middle of the night, a half moon rises in the southeast to cast a veil of blue light over the canyon.

DAY 2

Dawn breaks to an overcast sky and the roll of thunder in the distance. It's the monsoon, come to hound us from the Sea of Cortez.

After a quick breakfast we pack up and load the canoe. All the gear is stuffed into dry bags, stowed and lashed to the thwarts. Before long a thunderhead moves over the canyon, bringing lightning and a steady rain. We wait until the worst of it passes, then get ready to run the rapid.

We catch up with the current, floating down into the canyon and its raging cataract roar. A final tug of the hat and here we go. Enter left of the rock then fade to the right, dragging a paddle now to slow our momentum. The bigger rapids are spread out here and easily avoided. But the river narrows below, gaining force. The channel breaks hard to the left where the current funnels into a long run of rapids and falls we couldn't see from our perch the night before. Too late now. The full force of the river pushes us into the upper falls toward a wall of boulders at the bottom. If we run up on these rocks we're sure to flip. Down over the falls we go toward the boulders, bracing for the collision that seems imminent now, as the bow hits the hole and pivots against a wall of water backing up against the rock. The stern turns and rights itself, trim again with the current. We run past another hole and over a second falls, then ride it out through a chop of standing waves at the bottom.

We take a breath, get our bearings, and make for the eddy.

About thirty miles from here and some 130 years ago, John Wesley Powell approached the Gates of Lodore with four wooden boats and a crew of nine. He described what he saw at Lodore as alternately a "beautiful portal" and a "dark portal"—one leading to a "region of glory," the other to a "region of gloom." Major Powell, the first to navigate the Colorado River through Grand Canyon, knew what he was talking about. For us this morning in the rain and thunder, this verges on a canyon of gloom. Dark and foreboding. And while we're not out to explore any terra incognita, we understand that our journey is part of a different quest. Our blank spot on the map resides in the imagination, and right now it includes all the various things that could go wrong. It's sixteen miles to our camp at Harding Hole and another forty-six miles beyond that. We can expect rapids like this all the way down. There's no one coming along behind us, and any attempt to hike out promises to be long and difficult.

We've taken on water. With our coffee cups we bail out the canoe and continue down the rapids toward Little Joe. Thunder booms through the canyon as we have to pull over again to bail. At Little Joe, the river drops out of sight at the head of a long whitewater run. We find a place to land and walk down over the rocks until we can scout what's ahead. The current fractures here into a number of different channels. Giant boulders, which at high flows create massive holes, now are exposed. The current is fast and powerful, presenting no clear passage. There's a chance we can run this rapid all the way down, but there's a better chance we can't. We'll have to line it. Rosemarie takes the bowline as I take the stern. Together we inch the canoe along the rocky bar around boulders, down through narrow chutes. It's a slow process in the rain.

Eventually, we draw even with the big hole in the center, hop in the canoe, and take our chances through the lower rapids. The torrent rises and falls, changing directions through the rock garden. Our canoe bounces around the boulders, following a course not entirely unlike the one we had in mind. But we get through, take up the bail cups again, and get ready for Five Springs.

We've come a long way to be humbled like this, to be reminded once more of our precarious purchase here on planet Earth. Later, when a fair wind rises to chase the clouds east toward the seat of our empire, we'll have a chance to think about these things. Drifting along the shadow line beneath a towering rock wall, we'll consider what it is precisely that draws us to this. These same canyons that inspire reveries of delight in the sunshine become something altogether different in the rain and rapids. Today, it's lightning and deadly hydraulics—images of entire trees caught below the surface, twisting in the dark currents of deep channels. No question, this is a land of extremes. And yet we can hardly overlook our complicity in the process, the ease with which our perspective shifts with even the slightest change in conditions. How fickle and capricious our conceits finally seem. How tenuous our deepest convictions.

But, still, we know it's true: sometimes you *do* have to scare hell out of yourself for a little peace of mind. Twelve times the ocean has covered this place, Rosemarie will remind me. The world will end for us too, she'll say, just as it did for the dinosaurs. My partner. Who tells me that someday she wants to take scuba gear to Glen Canyon to explore what remains of the fantastic landscape buried now in all the water and silt. Says she's curious if there's anything to see. My beautiful partner. Who doesn't flinch when I tell her how many species go extinct every day in this world. Who says nothing to the fact that the world's human population will double in her lifetime. Who only smiles when I tell her that once there were places on earth that had never known a trace of human existence.

The rain has stopped. The sky looks brighter to the west. The canyon begins to assume its familiar colors: alabaster beaches, emerald wire grass, vermilion and ruby walls, sapphire sky. From here down we'll take it easy, go slow.

At Five Springs, I scout the whitewater from a standing position in the canoe. We decide to run it as is, relying on our skill to avoid the biggest hazards. Farther down at Big Joe we enter left of the exposed rock, then keep it steady through the lower chop. Above us, the banded bluff of Haystack Rock shines in the sky—white on top, red below. We'll bang rocks through these rapids and take on water, but we'll get through just the same.

We make our second camp at Harding Hole, a spacious park with a couple of side canyons leading out. But they'll have to wait because it's hot now, easily in the nineties. I commandeer the inner tube, lash the day cooler to the side with rope, and spend the better half of the afternoon in the circular flow of a large eddy. Starting at the top, I make a run down the riffle to the bottom where a few paddle strokes of the hand steer me back inside the whirlpool. The upstream current carries me to the top again where I begin the process all over. It seems I'm not the only one who has this idea. A half-dozen Canada geese enter the whitewater upstream to come ripping down the rapid along the far wall. They'll do this a couple of times, which leads me to believe there's no practical purpose in their behavior. Nothing of utility. Could it be they're just having fun? I thought of the avian family, only crows knew the pleasure of pranks and tomfoolery.

Later in the afternoon, when the heat of the sun subsides, we start for Johnson Canyon and the Indian ruins rumored to be scattered there. On a hillside covered with prickly pear and Indian rice grass, we find a most peculiar sign. Directly on top of a pile of deer pellets is an equally prodigious portion of the mountain lion variety. Cat scat on deer dung. And what does *that* mean? Good housekeeping? A gentle reminder of their respective positions on the food chain? Just another prank?

On our way back, we pause on the hill as the sun drops below the ridge. At night we find a hidden oasis above the beach and decide to sleep there…as the moon breaks through the trees and the northern crown fades into the galaxy.

Day 3

Today we'll float some fourteen miles of goosenecks on the Yampa before finishing with Warm Springs Rapid, the biggest whitewater on the river. But first there's Signature Cave to see at the bottom of Harding Park, only a mile or so below camp. We float to a sandbar and tie up. The cave (really an alcove) appears in the distance as a black oval set along a sandstone ledge overlooking the river. We start up the trail, as heat waves ripple over the desert floor.

Years ago, outlaw rustlers used Harding Hole to hide their stolen horses and cattle. In fact, this whole region enjoys a rich tradition of outlaws, bandits, assorted rogues and renegades. Just north of here is Browns Hole, erstwhile home to the Wild Bunch and its two most celebrated members, Butch Cassidy and Harry Longbaugh. Just down the Green a few miles is the Josie Morris cabin—homestead to Cassidy's onetime neighbor and eldest daughter in the renowned Bassett family. Josie's sister "Queen Ann," a wild one in her own right, was engaged to Matt Rush when he was shot and killed by the manhunter Tom Horn. By all accounts, Butch Cassidy was loyal, generous (an old Browns Hole resident recalls, "Cassidy did far more to redistribute the wealth in northwestern Colorado than Franklin Delano Roosevelt, and he did it a whole lot quicker, and without any red tape"), fun-loving, a world traveler, and train robber extraordinaire. Through all his exploits, Cassidy never killed a man. To this day, there is evidence to suggest that Cassidy was not the man shot with Longbaugh in Bolivia. Josie herself claims Cassidy died an old man in Johnny, Nevada.

The trail cuts through sulphur flowers, sagebrush, and greasewood. We follow it up to the sandstone ledge leading to the cave where a spring seeps out of the rock. The last few steps are a bit treacherous as we step across mud into the cool shade of the cave.

Inside, a sandy floor extends seventy feet back. The ceiling is thirty feet at its apex and curves down on both sides. It's dark in here, but not so dark that we can't see the hundreds of names, dates, and other odd symbols scribbled on the walls—testament to the waves of pilgrims who have passed this way. River runners, miners, horse thieves, Indians. Each with a different purpose, perhaps, but all passing through just the same. Somewhere in this web of graffiti may be the name of an outlaw or two, though I might not recognize it. Some markings are more conspicuous than others, like the *1939* painted next to the name of a noted river runner, boldly stroked in metal gray. But it all strikes me as a bit curious, these names and dates scratched on the surface of implacable bedrock. Like taking a glowing ember from the fire and writing your name across the night sky. The gesture strikes me as a bit absurd. And yet in a way maybe it's all we can ever really hope for, this accidental text. Literature, history, geology, rock art, the stars…all just fire writing in the dark. We read the signs as we find them, divine what we will, then try to locate ourselves accordingly. We do the best we can, sometimes braving it all to say, This is the world. This is who I am.

Back on the river, we enter the first turn in a series of goosenecks that will carry us down past Mathers Hole, Cleopatra's Couch, the Grand Overhang. For the better part of the day we'll let the current take us down, around, and back again through the long meanders. We're thirty miles and three days into the canyon now, and another three hundred feet down inside.

Well into river time.

For us, the goosenecks represent the heart of the Yampa and a chance to feel good and thoroughly lost. To recall senses numbed by a never-ending assault of concrete and glass. Senses weary from the grate and grid of neon and asphalt.

> Pull down thy vanity, I say pull down.
> Learn of the green world what can be thy place

Drifting along the edge of the river, we watch glints of liquid sunlight reflected on a rock wall. At the base of the wall, bubbles of river froth project onto the rock like amoebae under a microscope. Reminiscent too of the "heavy water light shows" from the old psychedelic days, my partner adds. Higher on the wall, the light becomes agitated like Richter spikes during an earthquake. Change the focus a little and the spikes level out into a neat pattern of sine waves, as by now I'm way lost in the enchantment.

Farther down we close our eyes, finding our way through a wilderness of sound: *te-yee, te-yee, te-yee, churrrrr*…modifying slightly, dissolving now with variation into a low amphibious *arrgghhh* downriver. A *plop* of sandbar that falls into the water. And behind it all, the ethereal ringing of deep quiet.

Up ahead three wood ducks fly in low, then skid across the calm, sunlit water in front of a rock wall in shadows. The coloration on the male is striking, auburn and white and iridescent green. Behind the ducks, a long lazy splash of reflected light blooms across the tapestry of canyon wall.

it is not man
Made courage, or made order, or made grace,
Pull down thy vanity, I say pull down.

Not far from here along the Green, Major Powell worked out many of his principles of geomorphology. The goosenecks are an example of what he and others called *entrenched meanders:* the winding oxbow bends of a river that are maintained as the land around them is uplifted. Powell recognized that a river always seeks a certain flow from its headwaters to its mouth. Specifically, it seeks a smooth and gentle profile with the minimum amount of current required to carry its material. This translates roughly into a gradient of one foot per mile. In the later stages of this eroding process, the river will cut a meandering course through valleys as it erodes sideward and widens the valley bottoms. The goosenecks of the lower Yampa represent a legacy of this process. The river has been able to maintain its serpentine course over millions of years, while the rock around it has uplifted.

At Grand Overhang we float along the edge of the river, peering a thousand feet up the rock face. We float just inside the shadow line as the sun's aurora swells in the blue sky above. A little farther, we gain the final neck and start the long straightaway to Katy's Nipple and Castle Park. The wind kicks up, as we find a rhythm (reach, dip, pull, and reach) in the teeth of the breeze. Just nine miles now to Warm Springs.

In addition to charting the landscape and developing his theories of geomorphology, Major Powell was busy naming things. Virtually all of the canyons on the Green, from the Gates of Lodore down, still bear the names he assigned to them in his journal. Some of these names, like Cataract and Whirlpool, describe geographic features. Others (Hell's Half Mile, Desolation) describe a landscape more personal in nature. An *interior* landscape. On our trip down the Yampa, we've encountered a distinct geography and a nomenclature to match—names like West Cactus Flat, Dry Woman Canyon, Cleopatra's Couch. Powell named a lot around here, but he didn't get to everything. So we try our hand at it. We've called a pillar of rock upstream from here Cobra Rock. Haystack becomes Shark Fin because that's what it looks like. When we float past Katy's Nipple we imagine how the rock was named, going as far as to reconstruct the scene: "We'll call it…Let's see, how long have we been out here in this *god-forsaken* wilderness?"

At Hell's Canyon, we tie up below the frontier cabin and make the half-mile hike to Mantle Cave. Archaeologists have been busy here, picking through ancient artifacts to paint a picture of Dinosaur's early inhabitants. The finds at Mantle Cave go back nineteen hundred years to the Fremont culture and a subsistence economy based on horticulture, hunting, and gathering. The Fremont lived year-round in these canyons, storing their produce of squash, beans, and corn in masonry granaries like the ones here in the cave. In this cave alone, archaeologists have uncovered six caches of artifacts including knives, spears, arrows, baskets, blankets, pottery, and a full-length headdress made from winter ermine and 350 flicker feathers.

But of all the finds in the Yampa caves, my personal favorite has to be the collection of suspender buttons, cartridge cases, and other odd items belonging to hermit Pat Lynch—the first white man to take up residence in these canyons. Pat and his gear were found by archaeologists under a clearly defined layer of silt and dirt. As with most everything else out here, it looks like he too was on his way to rock.

Before the Fremont, there existed a different class of Yampa denizens distinguished by their Archaic lifestyle. Beginning about 5,000 BC, when the Pleistocene megafauna went extinct, residents here became more dependent on the gathering of roots, seeds, and nuts to supplement their take of mule deer, bighorn, and rodents. They lived in pit houses built along the lower valleys during the winter months, moving to higher elevations in summer, and then to the forests in autumn where they collected pinyon nuts and juniper berries. Go back further in the archaeological record—as far back as 10,000 BC—and we find the earliest inhabitants of the Yampa canyons: a nomadic group of Paleo-Indians who followed the migratory herds of mammoths, giant bison, and camels.

Turn it all around, and you have an interesting human lineage of mammoth hunters, gatherers, farmers, trappers, outlaws, hermits…and now us.

Just four miles to Warm Springs when we float through Outlaw Park. Farther down, we notice an entire flock of bighorn sheep perched along the slope of the canyon. One of the adults bears a set of horns, as a duet of sorts passes between the bleat of a yearling and the throaty alto of an adult. We count as many as ten bighorn on the rocks between the outcrops and sage-brush. The river is slow and meanders through the steep canyon. We can see the high-water mark along the shoreline walls, reaching nearly six feet in plac-es above the current level.

The last gooseneck, a fleeting shadow from a passing raptor, and the long straightaway to Warm Springs comes into view.

We tie the canoe to a rock above the rapids and make our way to a scout-ing position above the big hole. Warm Springs Rapid was created in 1965 by a sudden influx of boulders into the river, the result of rain and a heavy slide down the draw. The rapid is hardly the raging monster it is at high water, but it's still dangerous—especially with all the exposed rock.

Looks like we can walk the canoe down even with the hole, then ride it out the rest of the way, careful to avoid those two widowmakers at the top. That's the key. Get hung up and turned sideways in this whitewater, and we're sure to go over. Once we're through the upper rapid, there's the rock garden below to navigate.

We make a final check to see that all the gear is lashed down, secure. I hold the stern line while Rosemarie scrambles over the rocks to a position just be-low the first big boulder. The force of the current pulls the canoe downriver. I let the rope out slowly, enough for her to grab the bowline. We ease the canoe down this way, trying to avoid the stronger currents in the main channels. We guide the craft over a falls between two rocks, and draw even with the big hole. Ready now, we take our seats and enter the rapid.

A quick stroke on the right to bring the bow in line and then a hard J-stroke left, *juuust* enough to skirt the hole and squeeze through the gap. Into the rock garden now, scraping bottom on a sleeper, turning sideways against the current. Spin, we must spin. Backpaddle hard, using the downstream flow to push us off the rock to get turned around in time for the pile of standing waves at the bottom, keeping an angled tack just off the tongue so as to roll over the waves. We clear the upper rapids and get ready for the lower run, cheating to the inside of the bend, allowing for the lateral push of the current. We see a passage and shoot it. The slap of standing waves recedes in the dis-tance. Sunlight glitters in the foam as we make for the calm. We're through Warm Springs.

The reward for all this is Box Elder Park. The sun is sinking fast, so we set up camp: river bags, cooler, chairs, fire pan.

A fish slurps the surface, as the sound reverberates off the canyon wall. I think about the "big double ugly" attractor I have in my fly box but decide to save it for another time. Another river. Still, I wonder who's down there. Humpback chub? Bonytail chub? Razorback sucker? Then again, maybe it's a Colorado pikeminnow, largest minnow species in North America, reputed to reach six feet in length. All of these fish are native to the Colorado River system, found nowhere else on the planet, and all are endangered. From dams, diversions, exotic species.

Dinner is on—lasagna, rolls, a delicate Chianti—as the bed of coals settles in the firebox.

Across the river, forty feet away, a high sandstone wall provides the acoustical backdrop for a secondhand guitar. To the occasional *crack* of hot embers, the strings are coaxed into loose arrangements. The notes sound crisp in this natural amphitheater. A bat splits the spiral of sparks circling above the fire, as the fingers walk a chromatic scale to the minor refrain. An old ballad rings fresh and new, before the coals burn low. Red to white, then to gray.

The high, arching walls of the canyon surround us, framing the universe in a window of stars. At one end of the window shines the bright light of Venus, falling fast. A shooting star streaks across the sky, and I make a wish.

As the northern crown dissolves into the Milky Way, we ponder space. The cosmos. How old? And these canyon walls. How old? And us: mere shadows of thought (something less) tied to gravity and biology, marooned here on this cinder of a planet whirling through space. The brightest star in the Corona Borealis is 75 light-years away, we're told, which means that the light we're seeing tonight was emitted in 1920. And what was happening then? Western civilization is still reeling from its European skirmish. O'Shaughnessy Dam is under construction in Hetch Hetchy Valley. Here on the Yampa, Nathaniel Galloway is busy refining his stern-first technique and flat-bottomed boat design.

Next to the Alpha star in the constellation is the Beta star, at a distance of 100 light-years. And then there's the Gamma star at 140 light-years away. That takes us all the way back to 1855. The first edition of *Leaves of Grass* is published. A young John Powell is plying the waters of the Des Moines, Ohio, Illinois, Mississippi. And out west, Crazy Horse is riding the northern plains, chasing his dreams and visions in this world made of shadows.

Another shooting star. Make a wish.

But to contemplate time, the immensity of it. (The river runs under a melody of crickets that just now changes key.) The mountain *knows,* the canyon walls *know.* They've seen it all before: hunter-gatherers, bullwhackers, one-armed explorers...deserts, jungles, oceans. The walls, the rock: silent yet somehow profoundly *there.* If only mostly imagined. Boulders tumbled into the river, canyon walls eroded down to be washed under oceans, raised in upheavals to be exposed and eroded again by the river...When? How long? My mind registers a number, but its significance is as elusive as the hole of time it tries to quantify.

Another shooting star, and I'm glad because there's one more thing I want to say.

One day when the soils are too saline to farm, the siltation too thick, the dams too precarious to hold, the river canyon will take care of itself in a way only it can. It may be a hundred years from now, maybe a million. But it will. The earth will endure, with or without us.

The canyon rock still holds the heat of the sun as my view of the galaxy blurs, then fades to nothing.

Day 4

I rise before the sun and wander back through the box elders where I surprise a big buck in velvet. I watch until he disappears through the trees before continuing on, scrambling up the long terrace of upland benches that eventually lead out of the canyon. Juniper trees grow along each bench. I climb high enough to gain a view of the river and return to my notes, re-creating the day before—the cave, Warm Springs, Box Elder—and *now* on the rocks. "I sit here on day 4 at Box Elder bar," I write, "above a broad beach of soft white sand and a 200-foot cliff across the river, watching a pair of ravens glide over the rim, recalling the glowing stripe of sunlight painted there the evening before, swallows chirping in the cliff hollows behind me, as I reconstruct Day 3 and Signature Cave..."

The canyon walls turn from russet to vermilion to fiery orange. I can see the camp below in the still gray of dawn.

Powell journeyed up the Yampa some "four or five miles," he wrote, from his camp at Echo Park all the way to Warm Springs. Not a small feat, if you consider the time of year (late June) and the high flows he must have encountered. He and his men made the trip twice. On the second excursion they climbed Mount Dawes, where Powell found a "monument" of stone that he thought may have been left by Francisco Silvestre Velez de Escalante, the Spanish priest who was here in 1776. Escalante, trying to establish a trail from Santa Fe to Monterey, is considered by many to be the first European to have seen the area. It seems that even Powell himself was aware of the web of signs into which he'd wandered.

There were others too before Powell. In 1825, General Ashley led a group of six trappers down the Green, from the mouth of the Big Sandy to the confluence of the Duchesne. Ashley and his men floated the river in bullboats and dugout canoes. He made the trip in part to open a southern route for his fur trade, using the boats to haul supplies since he'd already lost a number of horses to the Crow. Ashley started his journey into the unknown amid lively rumors of rapids, waterfalls, and one nasty suckhole, the latter courtesy of Jim Beckwourth. Beckwourth would later claim to have saved Ashley's life at Split Mountain—a claim refuted more often than not.

At a run of falls in Flaming Gorge, Ashley chiseled his name in a rock where it would be seen twenty-four years later by a band of bullwhackers on their way to the goldfields of California. This crew of forty-niners was led by a fellow named Manly. Tired of the dust and oxen, they split from their party and patched up a sunken ferry barge they found abandoned in the mud. Thinking that the Green would take them to California, they got as far as Ashley Falls where they marooned the craft on rocks. From there, they built a crude catamaran out of pine logs and continued down the river. They would build one more of these boats before they were done. Manly and his crew made it all the way through Gray Canyon before they were persuaded by a Ute chief to abandon the river and find another wagon train in Salt Lake City.

A thin braid of fire smoke rises from the beach. Camp is stirring. I finish my thought and return to the river.

Not a cloud in the sky this morning, and it promises to be hot. Very hot. A second pot of coffee is brewed and promptly laced with hefty doses of the foreign cordial we've brought along. Breakfast consists of granola and yogurt, topped off with a healthy dash of windblown river grit.

"Good for the gizzard," Rosemarie allows.

We count our cuts and bruises.

"Whoever has the most by the end of the trip," she says, "will have had the most fun."

Just a two-mile float to Echo Park today. Beyond that it's Whirlpool Canyon, Jones Hole Creek, and Island Park. As we float away from camp, the terraced wall behind Box Elder Park recedes in the distance. The river air remains still in this enclosed corridor of canyon. In this quiet corner of the world.

The view of Echo Park slowly unfolds behind Jenny Lind Rock. Farther down, Steamboat Rock marks the confluence with the Green. The flows are low and the mighty Green is nearly mistaken for a segment of the Yampa, but the clear color and swift current indicate otherwise. I recognize the scooped-out shell of Steamboat Rock ("like a blaze," I'll later write), and so I yell. The echoes return with resounding clarity, just as they did for Major Powell so many years before. Just as his words return to us now: "In some places two or three echoes come back, in other places they repeat themselves, passing back and forth across the river between this rock and the eastern wall…[like] magical music."

It was here in Echo Park that the major nearly met his demise. On his second day of camp—and we should remember that his narrative first appeared as a series of adventure stories for a popular magazine—Powell started out with another man, Bradley, to explore the area. Having lost an arm in the Civil War, Powell was clearly handicapped as a climber. Eventually, he became stranded on a cliff with nowhere to go, up or down. The resourceful Bradley, sensing the urgency of the situation, shed his drawers and dangled them below to the imperiled major. Powell then had to let go of his only handhold on the rock to seize the pants. He was able to execute the move and survived the ordeal unharmed. Bradley would later claim that the event took place much farther downstream. But by now it hardly matters. The incident was captured in a famous engraving and to this day remains firmly etched in the western imagination.

We float through the park, riding the current past long spits of sand, trying to envision an impoundment here against the walls that made Powell's "magical music" so many years before. But it's tough to imagine this place under eight hundred feet of silt and slack water. The color of the river is a dull olive, not exactly the "golden" hue ascribed to it by another noted western author, but then he too had his moments of rhetorical flourish. It seems to come with the territory, out here in the High West. Where it doesn't matter how you embroider your yarn, just so long as it's a good one.

More echoes.

Not so many years ago, Edward Abbey floated the Green south of here with a group of his friends. Along for the ride was the ghost of Henry Thoreau, keeping low and out of the way between the lines of a dog-eared copy of *Walden.* A kind of "canyon crank meets village crank." For Abbey, it was a chance to reacquaint himself with his philosophical mentor, to consider the significance of Thoreau's ideas in the late twentieth century, and to ruminate on just what Henry may have meant in some of his more memorable phrases. And there were plenty. But there's one in particular that comes to mind just now, one that returns again and again to haunt. *In wildness is the preservation of the world,* Thoreau wrote. In the trees, rocks, and canyons. The rivers, plants, and animals. And yes, the wildness in us. That which inside us responds to the natural world. That place in our hearts that registers the *flash* of recognition.

It's impossible for us to float through Echo Park and not think about what happened at Glen Canyon and all that was lost: Dungeon, Twilight, Mystery, Cathedral, Hidden Passage, Music Temple. And other places lost, too: Hetch Hetchy, High Spicer Meadows, Flaming Gorge, Bruce's Eddy, Pine Flat, Hungry Horse, Marmes Rockshelter...the rivers Stanislaus, Brazos, Allegheny, Kootenai, Coosawattee, Gauley, Feather, Tellico. All gone now. If not for the efforts of a few dedicated people in the 1950s, the same would be true of the Yampa. The successful preservation of this river was due in large part to the publication of a book, *This Is Dinosaur,* which argued the case for conservation. Not fifty years after the decisive victory at Echo Park, two major dams remain under consideration for the Yampa—one at Juniper, another at Cross Mountain. Either one of these would reduce the Yampa to a mere footnote in history, as the last free-flowing major tributary of the Colorado River to be damned.

The current winds around Steamboat Rock, cutting down through the heart of Mitten Park Fault. We float along the riffles and runs, past sandbars and islands.

At the entrance to Whirlpool Canyon, two massive outcrops tower above the river like twin stacks of black poker chips. Here, the canyon rises a thousand feet in the sky. Here, too, the record of millions of years: from the Late Cambrian strata of Uinta Mountain quartzite to the layered sheaths of dark Lodore Formation; higher still, above the junipers, a massive buff Madison layer; and at the very top, crowning the canyon, a light-gray precipice of Weber sandstone. The entire record is reflected in an instant across the placid calm of the river—a shimmering chronicle of the earth's history.

The canyons through here are every bit as striking as those along the Yampa. High fluted ridges fan down from above, falling hundreds of feet to the river like watery sand castles spun from the fingertips. Ponderosa pines grow in the most unlikely of places, on high benches suspended against the walls of giant amphitheaters. Boulders and deadfall choke the mouths of hanging valleys. Along one quiet stretch, the canyon walls drop straight down to the water in right angles, forming cozy alcoves at the edge of the river. We backpaddle into one of these shady retreats under a cascade of flowering fern. A spinning eddy keeps us in place, long enough to look straight up the wall into a whorl of sky. A stroke of the paddle starts us back toward the current, as a tiny vortex of water spins away from the canoe.

Yes, whirlpools.

Out of nowhere a massive roil of water breaks the surface, lifting the canoe upon its crown, stopping us dead in the middle of the current. The river here follows a pattern of short, intense rapids, segmented by quiet stretches of pools and drifts. With each rapid we have to read the waters to make a good, clean run. In many places, particularly at the bottom of rapids, the current flows between two giant eddies—like passing between Scylla and Charybdis.

But the river is swift, and it takes us little time to get down to Jones Hole Creek. This spring creek, named for Powell's photographer, has eroded away an impressive canyon between a wall of Weber sandstone on one side and a colorful Lodore Formation on the other. Along the bank, the river is cold and clear where a plume of springwater merges with the Green. We float past the rockbar and tie up below the mouth. A shadow darts under the canoe in the shallow current. Looked like the red arc of a rainbow, though it might have been the golden flash of a wild brown.

We have a few hours of daylight to burn, so we pack the water bottles and start up the trail along the fast creek that plunges and circles back on itself under the shady cover of box elder and willow. The path winds through a field of cheatgrass around pungent sagebrush, greasewood, and aster. There are alcoves in these hills, hollowed out of sandstone by ancient winds.

Two miles up, we leave Jones Creek for a narrow side canyon heading west. Ely Creek is only about two feet across and maybe six inches deep, but it supports a dense riparian growth. A quick scramble up the rocks and we make our way to the head of a waterfall, where the creek funnels through a groove of slickrock before plunging over the wall. We christen it Fat Ass Falls, on account of that's what's needed here to plug up the creek. Seated just so in the groove of the rock, a person can stop the falls and create a nice little pool at the top. A person can do this, that is, to the extent he can stand the frigid water.

After a brief wallow in the pool, we head back down Ely Creek to the panel of pictographs along Jones Creek. This wall, ten feet high and twice again long, depicts large square-shouldered figures wearing what look to be pronged headdresses. In other petroglyphs and pictographs that we find in the area, we'll see horned human figures, snakes, bighorn, vortexes, and other symbols that look downright alien. No one has come up with a definitive translation of these figures and symbols, though some appear to us, anyway, to convey a cosmological significance. Moonflower grows wild out here, and we can only surmise how much of this rock art was inspired by the psychoactive properties of native flora. On the other hand, it's hard for us to imagine a world devoid of cars, roads, fences, power lines, dams, ranger stations, NPS plaques...all the sights, sounds, and trappings of modern industrial society. How different the world must have seemed, even two centuries ago. The longer we're out here, the better we're able to unravel the layers of learned perception accumulated in our artificial environs. Layers that color the senses, shape the imagination. What secrets of the world did these people see that we cannot?

A blast of wind roars down the canyon and lets fly a half acre of dust and leaves. This has been the pattern lately: afternoon wind and clouds that dissipate at sundown. The hike has left us both a bit delirious in the hot sun. We take it easy on the way back, stopping regularly for water in the shady glens along the creek.

Back at the river, Rosemarie spies a trout hiding in the shallow water under the canoe, port-side aft. She sneaks to the back and leans over the gunwale, her long brown hair falling nearly to the water. She waits as the canoe drifts with the current, then lunges with her hands under the boat. The trout gets away, none the worse for the momentary scare.

The Green is faster now, though nothing like what awaits us below at SOB, Schoolboy, et al. At Compromise Bar we follow the right channel through the rapids, dragging paddle to stay off the wall, taking the opportunity to reflect again upon western place-names and what makes them so rich. So profoundly to the point. Behind the names is a particular attitude, forged in the thin air and vast spaces amid the extremes of light, weather, and geography that make the West so singular. *Compromise, Conundrum, Quandary, Paradox, Last Chance, Jack Ass*... all denoting a particular way of looking at things that seems to come naturally in this high desert country of mountains, canyons, buttes, and plateaus.

And once again we're reminded of the *textual* landscape that seems so conspicuous here: geologic strata, Indian pictographs, explorers' journals, desert varnish, metal paint, you name it. All of it a story to be read, a text to be untangled. And the river and canyons, all plenty big enough to accommodate the diverging perspectives. For Powell, it was a journey into a geographic and psychological unknown. For Indians, a land of sustenance. For Ashley, an avenue of commerce. For civil engineers, kilowatts. And for us... well, what? A kind of psychic resuscitation. A chance to feel the world again in our bones and blood. A reminder, perhaps, that all is not lost.

Below Greasy Pliers Rapid (*Greasy Pliers*?) the river enters Island Park, where the layered rock bends and breaks in a fantastic swirl of mountain, the result of uplift and warping. From here down, the current splinters into a maze of meanderings and intermittent channels. The idea here is to locate the swiftest run and ride it out as best we can. Deciphering a route is tricky, especially where the river flows around the islands—Buck, Big, Hog, Bobby, and Ford. Around the bend at Tree Island—not an island at all this time of year—we pass a stand of dead cottonwoods. From a distance, the black and white trunks look like haphazard piano keys planted in the ground.

This river corridor is an oasis for wildlife, attracting all kinds of species. On our float through Island Park we'll see beaver, deer, mergansers, and a large raptor roosting at the top of a skeleton cottonwood. Elsewhere we've encountered lizards, water snakes, bull snakes, otter, a variety of butterflies and birds, in addition to all those species we can't identify. Or see. Bear, bobcat, lion, etc. Meanwhile, one nefarious fly has lodged itself in the top of my foot, bringing me back to the business at hand. It slashes away at will, while I'm occupied for the moment with the paddle. I go after it with my other foot— once, twice, *three* times—until the only thing remaining is the sharp stinger still stuck in my skin.

The wind rises up to scour the beaches, chasing sand ghosts across the water. We float through Rainbow Park, where Powell was inspired by the colorful layers of rock sloping to the rim in "blue and lilac, buff and pink, vermilion and brown"...making for the portal to Split Mountain Gorge as the sun slips behind a rampart of clouds in the west, casting bars of golden light across the sky. It's been a long day. We keep on for the canyon and the inside protection of Moonshine Draw.

At the mouth of the canyon, a giant boulder splits the Green in two. The entire river narrows to about fifty feet. We stay to the right, avoiding the rock, and run the rapids into a big, sweeping eddy below. We're tired, it's nearly dark, and there's nothing but whitewater ahead. A beach slopes down to the river, and we decide to camp there.

We unload the gear, set up the tent near a brake of tamarisk, and drag the canoe high onto the beach. The river charges into the canyon here, and its power is not lost on us. Throughout the night I'll listen to the rapids and the sound of thunder in the distance, thinking about the seven miles of whitewater that lay ahead.

A desert wind blows down the canyon, feeling good beyond words. Later, when the moon appears, it casts a lacy shadow of tamarisk flower across the netting of the tent.

DAY 5

The sun eclipses the southeastern ridge as we break camp. Everything in dry bags for the final run out, lashed down. The last seven miles of the trip might be the most difficult of all, dropping twenty feet per mile. We wait for the sunlight to strike the top of Moonshine Rapid before pushing off—into the river the Spanish called the San Buenaventura.

The canoe drifts upstream in the eddy, circling around to the foot of the boulder and the entry to the main current. Once inside the rapids we cheat left, close to a gravel bar in case we need to pull over and scout. The flows are bigger here in the gorge, making navigation more difficult. Sometimes the hydraulic forces push us to places we don't want to go.

We enter Moonshine Rapid middle-left and float down, avoiding the bigger holes and hazards. Next up is SOB (not as bad as it sounds). We fade right near the gravel bar and run it out. The sun has climbed high enough now to illuminate the entire river. With the added light, we can see into the river to discern any snags or rocks "sleeping" below the surface. The advantage here may amount to only a second or two of extra time, but even this makes a difference.

The river narrows at the entrance to Schoolboy Rapid before dropping out of sight into a giant hole. Better scout this one. From the rocks above the rapid we see the boulder, the hole, the full scope and measure of Schoolboy. Too big to chance. We decide to nose the canoe down along the edge of a gravel bar past the hazard. Powell himself had a close call through here. He followed the same strategy of walking his boats around the bigger rapids.

Once we draw even with the hole, we hop in and ride the rest of it out. Schoolboy, like most of these rapids, is punctuated at the bottom by a long run of standing waves where all the various currents converge. These haystacks are tall and choppy, situated hard against the upstream flow of a powerful eddy. Enter sideways, or get caught on the edge of the currents, and the canoe is sure to flip.

At Lower Schoolboy, we tie up at a rockbar and scout again. We see nothing but exposed rock the whole way down, with no clear passage. The only chance seems to be along the far channel, but even that is risky. It will require a quick change of direction where the river turns sharply in front of a huge boulder. Question is, can *we* make that turn as well? The entire force of the river seems to be pushing toward the boulder.

But the sun is out in full glory now, and we've already run a number of difficult rapids. Confidence runs high.

We walk the canoe upstream, then paddle hard against the current to make our entry on the far side. Once across, there's nothing left to do but float down and wait. The river is bony and we skid over rocks, throwing the canoe off course. The current carries us directly for the boulder. Like Powell, we wait to be "dashed against the rock." And we are. The canoe climbs the boulder before we can fend off and turn the bow straight again with the current.

The river carries us down into a glassy pool at the bottom of the rapids where sunlight sparkles on the water. A hummingbird darts across the river and hovers above the canoe, close enough to see the ruby ring around its throat, the blur of wings. The bigger rapids are behind us now. From here down, we'll let the current take us the rest of the way through the heart of Split Mountain.

As river runners, we're trained to watch for hazards and read the flows for purposes of navigation. And we do. Good enough, anyway, to get us through the rapids. But after five days, the play of water and light begins to leave an impression on the *mind's eye*. So much so that we'll continue to see these watery images long after we've left the river—with our eyes closed, in our sleep, when we least expect it. Roils, riffs, swirling currents…a perpetual kaleidoscope of liquid light.

Below Inglesby, we notice the fresh prints of a mountain lion on a small beach. We follow its running gait to a circle of geese prints, where the cat tracks come to a screeching halt. Right where the geese have been. We peer up into the harsh landscape of rock and cactus. The lion is up there somewhere, maybe looking down on us this very moment.

We're trained to look for hazards and currents, yet there are moments on the water when we feel the inclination to do otherwise. To engage in a different kind of reading. There are times on the river when the sun and water are just right, and the burnished walls of the canyon come alive in the reflective riffles and pools. It might seem then that we're on the verge of something *else,* some other way of seeing the world beyond the familiar realm of perceived phenomena. By then we will have stopped watching for rocks and channels. By then too, perhaps, whatever it was we thought to see will have already passed.

4. *In Deep at Wolf Creek*

We'd heard about Wolf Creek for some time, though it's hard to say what could have prepared us for all that we found there—certainly nothing in my experience to compare with the icy drive that first night over the pass, with the high white peaks all lit up under a full moon to fire the imagination and put that old familiar hole in the stomach whenever there's some formidable challenge ahead. Particularly when that challenge involves some risk. And there was nothing to prepare us too, I suppose, for the gamut of emotions a backcountry skier experiences in those rare times when he or she knows they're in it deep.

Wolf Creek Pass is truly one of the more spectacular places for telemark skiing, providing all the best the sport has to offer. It has outstanding descents, it enjoys the most snow in Colorado, and there's nothing fashionable about it. As much as all of this is true, Wolf Creek is also a place of the imagination—a place where a backcountry skier can chase wild notions about himself and the world. There's no doubt that we've come to Wolf Creek in a kind of pilgrimage to the fabled conditions this place is known for. At the same time, I know I'm here out of some vague and half-articulated desire to back both dreams and demons into a corner just to see what's there. For, aside from the sheer joy of skiing untracked powder in the backcountry, there is the strange compulsion here to engage the elements in some direct and meaningful way.

It's been snowing here for days, but the morning breaks clear and bright on this first day of spring. From town, the view of the pass is breathtaking. High, jagged peaks cut a blue silhouette against the dawning sky.

We follow the road east through the San Juan River valley, past horse ranches and ponderosa stands tucked neatly along the bends of the river. At the head of the valley the road makes a sudden switchback up the mountain. From here to the pass, the grade is extreme. Canyon walls tower in improbable verticality. We see only one other vehicle on the way up, a mud-splattered pickup truck with a bumper sticker that reads: *Shut Up and Ski.*

After a long climb, we park the car at the top of the pass and gather the gear. In our packs we'll carry food, water, knife, tools, wax kit, and extra clothing for the ski down—outer shell, gloves, and hat. Snow shovels get lashed to the outside of the packs. Joining me at Wolf Creek is my friend and backcountry partner August Chance. We lace up the boots, tie on the gaiters, and we're set to go.

As the first ones out this morning we have the arduous task of breaking trail. And while this can be a thankless job, it also means we'll ski untracked powder. I fasten the bindings and lean into a glide. The snow is dry and cold, but with the strong springtime sun overhead, this should all be different by the end of the day. We strike out across the near meadow for the trees where we begin our initial ascent.

Telemark skiing takes its name from the area of Norway where the technique was first developed. In 1868, Sondre Norheim introduced the tele turn at a ski-jumping event in Oslo when he knee-dropped into a graceful, arcing glide after landing an impressive seventy-six-foot jump. Norheim had perfected the turn in the hills near his hometown of Morgedal in the Telemark region of Norway. Given the free-heel bindings and wooden boards that skiers used back then, the technique proved not only stylish but functional. Executed properly, the telemark turn could approximate the action of one long, side-cut ski that worked especially well in deep snow.

The Norwegians brought their Nordic technique to America in the nineteenth century, but it wasn't until the early 1970s that telemark really caught on here as a few skiing purists, dissatisfied with the conditions at lift-service areas, looked to the backcountry for an alternative. Free-heeled gear allowed them to tour out-of-bounds, while the telemark turn provided the technique to negotiate steep descents. In places like Crested Butte, backcountry tele-mark skiing was rediscovered. For some skiers, it marked a welcome return to the sport's beginnings. It also had something to do with lifestyle. Backcountry telemark represented an independent way of doing things that appealed to many on philosophical grounds.

The hike to the top of the mountain is only about a mile long, but it gets steep in places and requires a bit of effort in the deep snow. We take our time and enjoy the morning—the snow-covered alpine firs, the pristine meadows, the curious ravens trailing shadows over snowfields. Halfway up, we're forced to traverse a long, open chute. We cross it one at a time, cutting a track into the steep angle of the slope. The ski area on the other side of the pass is blasting this morning, and we can hear the reports loud and clear, can even feel the shock waves in the air. Once, I feel the *wump* of a submerged snow layer collapse beneath me.

But the snow holds and we continue on, switchbacking up the next half mile into a windblasted snowscape of frozen drifts and dales. What few evergreens persevere out here are stunted and disfigured, but awful hardy just the same. In and around the snow swales we go, until a vista unfolds and the nameless mountain levels out. We ski around the wind-whipped drifts to the far end of the summit and the first drop on our backcountry run. We pick a leeward enclave behind a stand of fir trees, stamp down the snow, and get ourselves ready for the ski down.

From the top of the mountain, we can see the ski area to the south in the distance. To the east, visible along the horizon, the white serrated band of the Sangre de Cristos shines in a crystalline dome of blue sky. On a windless twenty-degree morning, the Sangres look absolutely stunning. Few mountain ranges inspire the way they do, especially on a day like this with a tantalizing dose of spring in the air. Turning to the north and west, the high alpine country rolls away in gulches, chutes, and swatches of fir. From here to the Uncomphagre Plateau bucks some of the most rugged country in all the West: the La Garitas to the north, the La Platas and San Miguels to the west, and the dramatic Sneffels, Needles, and Grenadier ranges in between. Mountain ranges whose crowning peaks bear such names as San Luis, Handies, Redcloud, Nebo, Sunlight, Windom, and Sawtooth. This too is one of the few places in the Lower 48 still big and wild enough to accommodate Griz. *Ursus arctos horribilis.*

The skins are stripped and packed away. Rifling through the gear, I grab my shell as we make final preparations for the ski down. A quick look at Chance and I see that he is ready too. Below us lies a hillside of fresh, uncut powder with what appears to be a deep and solid base. The conditions seem ideal, but neither one of us dares to say it. It's not often a fellow gets to feel holy, no sense spoiling it with a couple of shallow superlatives. The surface of powder sparkles in lilac, sapphire, and tangerine. It's deep, well over the knees, and looks light enough to be cottonwood down. I cinch up the tension ties, check zippers, batten all hatches. We pause at the top of the ridge, look for an opening in the trees, and drop over the edge.

Not ten turns off the top and I'm hopelessly lost in a fantastic maze of frosted alpine firs. A fresh foot and a half of powder blankets the low, sloping boughs as I ski through the trees—choosing my way as I go, following the course that looks best, all the while getting deeper and deeper into the heart of the maze and that prickly question of why do this at all. The snow beneath my skis is deep, perhaps twelve feet or more. It's all I can do to break the spell of floating through this enchanted forest. But avalanche danger is high, and there's the little business of not knowing where the hell I am. I stop and peer around the closest tree for Chance. I shout his name, but the word is absorbed into the thick walls of snow before it can even turn the corner. Talk is cheap up here, where the slender firs tower in a sky so blue it hurts just to look at it. A high branch releases its load of powder, starting a veil of glittering snow dust through a bar of golden sunlight.

As I blink, to sigh.

The question invariably presents itself to the backcountry skier what it is precisely that drives him out here, to go to all this trouble for a day of skiing recreation. After all, one doesn't have to do this. The fact of the matter is that people die at this sort of thing. Most, I think, would agree that the reason for getting into the backcountry has less to do with the courtship of danger than with something else. Given the choice, Chance and I would just as soon spend the day without the specter of avalanche hanging over our heads. But this is part of the deal, and we both know it.

I ski deeper into the maze. The trees are spaced far enough, perhaps five feet, to comfortably negotiate a string of tight telemark turns. It's a little steep at first, but once inside this maze it's not so bad. I find that if I keep a mental bead through the trees, a nearly unconscious one at that, the uncertainty of not knowing what's around the tree makes the experience all the more intriguing. But this works only if I stay loose. If I don't *think* about it too much.

Like any art form, there is a special satisfaction and reward to the mastery of telemark skiing. And we could easily leave it at that, if cutting graceful turns in a scenic wilderness were all there were to backcountry skiing. But the truth is, something else drives us out here to the geographic backbone of the continent. What lurks there in our tangled and tortured psyches? What genetic baggage left over from the days of sabertooths and woolly mammoths?

Consider it.

How much do we actually experience ourselves anymore, and how much is done for us by machines or vicariously through other people? Obsessed with removing every last vestige of risk from our lives, we've successfully sealed ourselves off in a thoroughly *simulated* existence. Cashed in our souls for a safer, more convenient option. In a time when our existence is highly symbolic and who we are is defined as much as anything by image, skiing this mountain might very well be the most ritualistic thing I can think of. It's the best way I know to make contact, to make a meaningful connection with the world. We don't have to do this, it's true. But the alternative seems even more terrifying.

Time to stop. Find Chance. Get our bearings.

Through a passage in the trees I catch a glimpse of his black coat and wave him down. It turns out that he's been yelling for me too, but likewise to no avail. This is truly a remarkable place. The snow sparkles in the morning sun. The air is bright and clear, the light as pure as any I've seen. Streaks of snow dust flash in the forest as they fall through sunlight. The trees look big, thirty feet high, but it's really only the *tops* of the trees that we see in all this snow.

We continue down through the glade, skiing through the deep cloud of powder. The idea here is to follow a general route of about three miles, dropping a total vertical descent of two thousand feet or so. All things being equal, we'll come out on the highway some four miles east of the pass below the snowshed. The plan is to hitchhike back to the trailhead and repeat the run until we've had enough.

The glade opens out finally at the head of a large north-facing bowl with a nice forty-degree pitch. We stop and look over the edge, neither of us stating the obvious. What one feels at a moment like this is a kind of emotional chaos: pure joy at the sight of something so enticing, and unspeakable fear at the thought of having it all go wrong. Given the pitch and the two or three feet of fresh snow, avalanche danger is real. But we see no signs of previous slides. As far as we can tell, the conditions look safe.

Chance takes his shovel and cuts a cross-section of snowpack. The snow is cold and dry, with a layer of depth hoar forty inches below the surface. Plenty deep and stable, it would seem. Standing in the shadows of the forest, we stare at the uncut powder glittering in the sun below.

"What do you think?" I ask.

Chance is not one to talk much, but a quick glance tells me what we both already know.

"Just stay close to the fall line," he says. "We'll go one at a time."

We traverse through the woods to where the meadow dips in the shadows before breaking off steeply near the bottom. We look for coordinates to help locate our lines in the event of a slide. The longer we wait, the more the anticipation works on us. I take a last breath and lean over the edge.

The snow is light and consistent. I cut one turn, another, and it's not long before the reflexes take over and I lock into the mechanics of technique and form. The turns lead one into the next in precise rhythm, so easily do the skis move through this waist-deep powder. If only for a moment I catch a glimpse of myself enjoying myself skiing this meadow. It seems as though I'm not skiing at all, but rather *floating* through some fantastic dreamscape. I can virtually see the lines of my submerged skis, feel the powder as it flies up under my chin, can even focus on the individual refractions of light on the surface of snow.

As fast as it began, the run comes to an end. My heart races as I wait at the bottom of the hill. I can't see my tracks above the last rise in the meadow— only the bottom few curves of a telemark line and the wake of powder where I've plowed through the snow, the dark shadows of the woods at the top, and a hole of blue sky above that.

Chance sails in beside me. He stops and waits, puffing clouds of white fog. This is just too good for words. The power of the experience resonates in the cells, and now the moment is stored in the bones of memory. Sometimes a skier can be so focused on what he's doing that he doesn't consciously recognize his exhilaration until the moment passes. It may take all of a second for this to happen, but he'll come to know the experience as something purely visceral, a *feeling*. Good, hard skiing is not at all unlike the sensation one gets upon coming out of a dream—that space of time in which dreamer becomes conscious of both dream and waking. The further the dream slips away, the more compelling it seems to the point that its residual effect will appear as real to him as anything he may encounter in his awakened state. In fact, much of the day will be spent in this kind of suspended state between dream and consciousness. Between the euphoria of the moment, and the conscious desire to recapture it.

From the meadow we make a traverse east through the trees, using the draw below to gauge our position. Our topo map tells us that if we venture too far south we could wind up in a gulch that looks extreme and prone to slide. Better to stay in the trees and make our way eventually through a lower drainage. Skiing trees is usually a safe way to go, as much as any of this is. Protected from the degrading effects of wind and sun, the snow stays fairly consistent without the kind of wind slab or crust typically found in exposed areas.

We continue on until we come to a long, knee-deep drop through the trees. The slope is about thirty-five degrees, enough to get a good head of steam through the powder. There looks to be a solid base underneath and enough snow to cover any snags or boulders that might be in the way. In fact, the only snags out here today are of the mental variety, glitches in concentration, which fortunately are few and far between. We each pick a route where the trees open out a bit, chart a course in our minds, and drop down.

On any given day there are a number of elements that can factor into a backcountry run: snow conditions, weather, terrain, equipment, stamina, frame of mind, even the company you keep. The slightest trepidation or distraction can disrupt your rhythm. Go too slow and you stick if the snow is too wet or fall through a weak base, which, if your speed is right, will send you cartwheeling down the mountain. Go too fast, and before you can stop yourself, every fiber in your body is stretched to the limit to regain control. The satisfaction of skiing depends heavily on technique and form. To be successful at this, a skier has to instantly process loads of information—on navigation, tack, conditions—and consistently make the proper adjustments. At the same time, he's got to stay loose. You can't be looking too far ahead or thinking about something that's already happened. Fixate on anything too long and you lose the rhythm. Of course, all of this wisdom is earned the hard way, only after countless hours of failure and frustration.

Breaking through the last of the trees, we cut the run off where the terrain begins to lose its pitch. We come to a stop in the middle of a small clearing where we take a few minutes to catch our breath. Collect our thoughts. Out in the open, the snowfield is a vision of brilliant light. We can feel the solar radiation rising off the snow. Behind us, our tracks wind thirty turns up the mountain through lodgepoles, trailing off in the distance. We find the symmetry pleasing—a satisfaction rooted, no doubt, in some kind of cheap vanity. But we hardly care. Not if the thing is done right. Besides, there's a feeling one gets out here that everything is in its place, as it should be. It's a feeling that could easily lead one to believe there is a purpose to things. A kind of innocence, really. The high country will do that to you. There's nothing like going face-to-face with a mountain to help clear your mind.

What we see of the San Juans today is primarily the result of an intense period of volcanic activity dating back forty million years to the Tertiary period. The volcanoes that erupted here spread vast deposits of lava and ash over the region, in some places as high as ten thousand feet, before settling out. This activity, centered mainly in the area north and east of the Needle Mountains, was so profound as to empty the magma chambers under the volcanoes, causing them to collapse. Evidence of these collapsed volcanoes can be found today in the fifteen or so calderas that have been identified in the San Juan region. The volcanoes of the Tertiary were then followed by glaciers of the Quaternary that created the U-shaped valleys, cirques, and carved peaks of the region. Add to this a million years or so of weathering and erosion, and one begins to get an idea of how this landscape was shaped.

As much as we talk about the local geology, we should also consider the broader context of plate tectonics and forces of compression caused by the North American and Pacific plates colliding into each other, the result of which can be seen in the tilted and wrinkled continental crust stretching from the Sierra Nevada across the Great Basin to the Rocky Mountains. Indeed, the San Juan uplift is composed of two basic structural elements: the ancient Uncomphagre arch running northwest to southeast and the more recent transverse belt of fractured coast known as the Mineral Belt. What we see finally is a landscape tempered by the forces of continental drift, fire and ice, wind and rain—all converging at a crossroads of space and time. In this particular moment that seems to branch out in all directions.

Into the trees again and across the mountain, time to move on. Another traverse, another meditation. Another facet on the gem of backcountry skiing.

We make our way east along the slope, keeping a high tack through the trees, taking our time to enjoy the sun and solitude. By now it appears that we can continue this strategy of traverse and descent until we simply run out of mountain. We make our way through the lodgepoles to a growth of young aspen trees, the result of a recent avalanche, it would seem. On a steeper slope we notice how the lower branches of all the trees have been sheared away. By slides, no doubt. Impressive as these signs are, the firm base and cold air both point to stable conditions. Our biggest concern today is that warming temperatures could eventually melt the surface between snow layers. With all their intricate variations of points and edges, snow crystals can readily attach themselves in a cohesive unit. As the crystals melt, they lose their structural integrity and become loose like roller bearings. This is particularly dangerous along the interface between two distinct snow layers.

We continue the traverse until another long run opens for us through the trees. We stop to make all the equipment adjustments: coat, glove shells, zippers, ties. I run the skis in place to free any snow clinging to the bottom. A deep breath, and down we go.

Around that important first turn, and we're quickly into the dynamics of the run—the angle of descent, contour of mountain, response of equipment, the depth and consistency of snow…all accounted for at the cutting edge where ski meets snow. Dropping now through the glade, as the mountain falls away to a steady rhythm of turn, lift, and turn. Balance, control, *poise*. Free-heeling through the trees, bending low through the turns so as to be nearly eye level with the surface of powder—like plowing waist deep through an acre of sparkling sea foam.

We keep at it through the forest, fighting back the pain until the quadriceps begin to burn. The same desire that can make a skier shake with anticipation is mobilized now to offset the stress. We break out of the trees into the sunshine and another open meadow, featureless in the blinding light. The inside of my glasses fogs up, and my eyes can't immediately adjust. For a second or two I lose all depth perception; the mind sees in two dimensions what the body skis in three. The knees buckle, then drop, as I barely navigate an unanticipated rise in the meadow. As the world falls away beneath my feet.

There's a balance to all of this, between attacking the mountain on one hand and being amenable to the conditions and vagaries of the terrain. By carving up this veneer of snow in highly stylized turns, we pay homage to the mountain and the feeling it allows us to have. It's as close to a feeling of belonging in the world as any I've known, the closest we may ever come to anything overtly religious. We ski the mountain for the chance to be on our own, for the challenge and sense of purpose it affords, and for the satisfaction in doing something well. Out here, we get a perspective on the world that we just can't find in town. It's here that we can begin to take some measure of who we really are. There comes a time when you have to look at everything with an even eye. The mountains, the sea, the grizzly bear and tick. These things simply *are*, in a world the origin and purpose of which perpetually elude us. As we, by virtue of some evolved faculty, remain blessed and cursed to ponder the paradox.

Out of the whiteout now, the fog clears. The eyes adjust. Chance has stopped just short of a crooked crease in the snowfield and what looks to be a covered creek bed. I cut one last sweeping turn and swing in beside him. The long run has worn us out. Doubled over the poles, we take a moment to rest. Glasses fogged, snow clinging to his beard, Chance is a study in economy: 70/30 shell, wool mittens, scuffed leather boots, decent single-camber skis, poles that don't match though both have baskets. Nothing frivolous or fancy. Just good basic gear.

Shut Up and Ski, it all seems to say.

As we guessed, the crease at the bottom of the meadow is a snow-covered creek that we'll have to cross. It's deep and wide enough not to be taken lightly. We scout out the biggest snow bridge in sight and ski one at a time, Chance taking the lead.

If we work at it, we can stay high enough on the north-facing slope to allow ourselves one last plunge through deep powder. We ski east through the trees, staying high on the slope. A Clark's nutcracker heralds our passing, but otherwise it's quiet out here, with only our own sounds to contemplate: the *skrinch* of boot sole against a metal toe plate, the *whoosh* of skis through snow, an occasional deep sigh in the thin alpine air. There is simply no other place we'd rather be right now. Nothing else we'd rather be doing.

Down again, on this last descent through the trees and the ski-out along the bottom of the drainage. This particular drainage, one of thousands in these mountains, is apparently too obscure to warrant a name. Still, it's more than a mile long from its source at the base of the Divide to its confluence with Pass Creek. Farther down, Pass Creek joins other creeks to form the South Fork of the Rio Grande. The South Fork then flows northeast out of the San Juans, merging with the Middle Fork to begin a long, ponderous flow through the San Luis Valley south to Taos and beyond, eventually emptying into the Gulf of Mexico. Not a stone's throw from where we started at the pass, Wolf Creek itself begins as a mere freshet—turning south to meet up with the West Fork of the San Juan River, joining the East Fork down below in the valley. On its way west, the San Juan is fed by the likes of the Piedra, Los Pinos, Animas, La Plata, and Mancos, all flowing toward their ignoble end at the big backwater called Powell.

At this lower elevation, the snow has already begun to soften. By the end of the day it will approach a consistency close to wet cement, but for now we think only of the dry powder that still remains higher up. We string together a final few turns through the trees, as the mouth of the drainage comes into view. At the bottom of the run we release the bindings, take off our skis, and make ourselves presentable on the road.

In no time at all, we'll thumb down a truck that will take us back up the road through the snowshed and over the pass to the trailhead. There, we'll sit on the tailgate of our car and look out across the *shining* mountains, enjoying a lunch of sandwiches, dried fruit, and chocolate bars, topped off by a couple of murky home brews. We'll make this ski circuit twice more before leaving the San Juans at sundown for points west, where we'll spend the night under the stars in pinyon and juniper country. In the morning we'll rise early and drive the car as high as it can take us into the La Sal Mountains. From there, we'll strap on the skins and skis and hike higher still, until we can look out over the red-rock canyon country of the Colorado Basin.

We'll spend the day skiing the bowls and glades of the high La Sals, where big Thoreauvian eyes watch from the trunks of aspen trees. Alone in the high country, trading comfort and convenience for the chance to catch the mountain and snow at just the right time. Wolf Creek today, the La Sals tomorrow. Who knows, maybe the Henrys next. Keeping west, one step ahead of the developers and boosters bearing down now on the tiny hamlet of Moab. Looking harder and harder for the unpeopled places. The untracked snow.

Chance sighs. *Ah well*, he says.

But he's not been listening. Not to me, anyway. I turn and see that he's been watching the runnel of snowmelt between his boots, running for the Pacific. Sometimes I forget that my partner doesn't rile the way I do. Just as well, I suppose. After all, there's the beer to finish, the ravens to watch, melting snow to listen for. Soon there'll be muscles to stretch. Skis and skins to strap on. A hike to make to the top of a continent, and the start of another backcountry run.

5. *Summer Ski*

As it pertains to the art of independent adventure, even the most casual observer cannot fail to recognize the interesting relation between the experience of an adventure and the story that's later told about it. To illustrate the point, consider the curious tendency by which the *glory* of an outside adventure will often grow over time in direct correlation to the distance one gains from the actual event. Depending on the skill with which the event is narrated, and to a lesser degree the feat itself, the adventure may even achieve near-mythic proportions. What this suggests, of course, is that it (glory) is by nature derivative and thus invariably false. In fact, in moments of rare clarity it will dawn on the amateur adventurer that what he is doing is really quite absurd, even insane, and that if he were to fully study the matter he would surely see that the real reason for risking his neck is a whole lot scarier than any physical harm that might come to him—although that can be pretty bad, too.

But that's another story.

What concerns us here is this adventurer's tendency to see things, himself included, in a decidedly skewed fashion. Tilt that eye far enough, as he usually will, and the entire business can even seem like fun. I mention all this only by way of introducing something I once proposed to Chance, namely, that we climb one of Colorado's highest peaks just so we could turn around and ski back down. As this idea didn't immediately appeal to him, he told me as much.

"It's going to take more than those old worn-out notions of glory and conquest to get me up that mountain," he said. "All for a mile or two of uncertain
skiing."

After thinking it over a while, I suggested that we wait until the summer
solstice. Then I started in about the mechanics of metaphor in Proust's "blue
flame of a violet"—how the juxtaposition of different events from different time periods reveals a common essence, effectively liberating each from
its temporal contingencies. Chance looked at me sideways, like maybe I had
gone too far. But the longer I went on, the more the idea seemed to make
sense to both of us, until we couldn't help ourselves. We pictured a sharp metal edge carving mountain ice under the longest sun of the year. We dreamed
of snowfields and snow flowers. We even went as far as to imagine a special
significance to the splendid unlikely. That is to say, an élan of incongruity.

At 14,265 feet, Quandary Peak is the fourteenth highest mountain in Colorado and the seventeenth highest in the contiguous United States. On the
morning we arrive, its white summit towers in a turquoise sky as a Melissa
Blue butterfly glides across a wild strawberry patch in full bloom. On this
first day of summer, there are dandelions and parsley too. Quandary sits on
the southern edge of the Tenmile Range, just north and west of the Continental Divide. To get to the top, we'll have to hike three miles and ascend
more than three thousand vertical feet. I glance in my friend's direction and
see that he is ready to go. We slide the skis into the slots of our packs, and begin the long walk to the summit.

Chance is decked out today in wraparounds, fedora, and Bavarian breech-
es. He wears a hawk feather in his hat just for the effect. I start off simple:
shorts, sneakers, sunblock. We prod our way with ski poles up an old mining road past the tumbledown remains of an abandoned shaft. It feels good
to be on our way. There's always a bit of anxiety involved in the preparation of
something new like this. It has a lot to do, I think, with trying to account for
the unknown. I have learned over the years to expect this anxiety, even to welcome it. If I'm nervous before a new adventure, then I take it as a good sign.
If I'm not, then I'm convinced this is reason enough to begin worrying.

In the subalpine forest of spruce and fir, the climbing gets progressively
steeper. And tougher. The wind gusts, pushing against our packs, and it

becomes apparent that any expenditure of energy should be carefully calculated to yield maximum efficiency. Beside the trail, a pool of water reflects the white clouds and blue sky above.

"Heaven on earth," Chance says with a grin.

Some of this initial anxiety might also have to do with coming to terms with one's destiny. As much as our decision to be here is a conscious one, we also recognize that there's something necessary about all of this. We don't fully understand it except to say that it has something to do with our peace of mind. As crazy as it sounds, we want to see if skiing in summer will change our perception of either one of these, simply by experiencing both in a new and different light. And while we do what we can to prepare for what might happen, we also accept the fact that we can never account for everything. We can never know entirely what to expect. The sense of destiny extends beyond just what we look forward to. It also includes everything that we don't look forward to. Or can't.

Rising through the last of the storm-blasted trees, we step onto a colorful carpet of alpine tundra. Tundra—from the Lappish word meaning "land of no trees"—refers to those major ecosystems found above mountain timberlines and beyond the latitudinal limits of tree growth. Amid the extremes of erosion, drought, cold, frost, wind, and sun, these delicate plants survive in a thin boundary zone between the air and ground. For only a few short weeks in June and July, they blossom in a stunning display of color and fragrance. Tundra wildflowers—resilient enough to withstand hard frosts even in bloom—may take decades, even centuries, to recover a damaged site. Chance surveys the vista to the north, while I ponder a ten-inch mat of dwarf clover that could easily be twice my age. Beside it are purple phlox and forget-me-not, maroon kittentails and yellow aven. I bend down for the alpine primrose, searching for the one fragrant blossom in the cluster of magenta and gold flowers.

Beyond the world of wildflowers, cloud shadows creep across spacious South Park on the other side of Hoosier Pass. To the east, the Blue River valley dips below a band of snow-crested peaks: Bald, Whale, Teller, and Grays. Because of a number of late-season storms, a threat of avalanche remains in the high country. Lightning too is a concern, especially above tree line.

The trail rises from the tundra to a boulder field just below the snow. We step across slabs of granite streaked with feldspar and quartz. A patina of lichen covers much of the rock in shades of lime, ocher, silver, and black. We proceed across the boulders to a high plateau, staying along the ridge that angles up to the summit as the wind blows against our packs and high-waving skis. During one particularly stiff gust, Chance has to stop and adjust his fedora. The conversation turns to geology, and he astutely recalls that momentous event when the "schist hit the alluvial fan . . ."

From here to the summit, the hiking gears down. We settle into a slow trudging pace, leaning weight into the wind. Above the plateau the trail enters the snow-covered high ground—a welcome reprieve from the treacherous boulders, until I posthole through the crust and sink up to my thigh in snow. Although this might not sound like an enviable position, it actually wasn't too bad. Anchored to the mountain like this, I was temporarily relieved not only from the rigors of climbing but also from the constant vigilance in the face of a swirling wind. In fact, I took a moment to reflect on our situation and to notice the details of our surroundings—the intense sunlight, the consistency of snow, the circling vultures overhead—because we weren't just hiking up this mountain. We were also thinking about it as we went along. And we were thinking about it in a way that would make sense to us later when we looked back on it. I have often felt that the course of my life has largely been predicated upon what I thought at the time would make a good story later on. To forget the details of an event, or to later dismiss them because they sound too incredible to believe, is in many ways to defeat the whole purpose. A fellow like Proust could understand this, I'm sure.

After a tough two-and-a-half-hour hike, we reach the summit of Quandary Peak. And what a view it is. For hundreds of miles, it seems, columns of clouds scud across snow-crested peaks. To the west, the terrain recedes in retrograde relief from the Gore Range in the north to the Sawatch Mountains in the south. Tennessee Pass splits the headwaters between the Eagle and Arkansas rivers—one bound for the Gulf of California, the other for the Mississippi Delta. Meanwhile, the headwaters of the Blue wait in two artificial impoundments at the base of our mountain, a thousand feet below. A raven sweeps the summit and I follow it over the edge, experiencing a wave of vertigo to go along with the delirium of altitude.

We break for lunch in the leeward pocket of a cairn as the sun slips behind a high cumulus cloud, creating a colorful halo of refracted light—a rainbow corona of pink, aqua, and violet. Chance kicks a small clump of snow and watches as it tumbles down a slope, gaining speed, its path and direction growing more manic as it shrinks and accelerates finally into oblivion, the idea of it rolling on ahead.

But it's cold at the top, the wind howls incessantly, and it's not long before we move off the summit to the head of the snowfield. At fourteen thousand feet, the snow on Quandary is whipped into frozen sastrugi. We clip on the skis and start down past a Clark's nutcracker picking ladybugs off the ice. The slope is less than thirty-five degrees, but fast. Tricky, too, with the slushy waves and inconsistent base. The terrain opens up, and I descend two hundred feet or so before my thighs begin to burn in the thin air. The snow grows softer below the summit, and sometimes we have to surf through the turns.

At the bottom of the snowfield we pause to rest. Below us, a maze of exposed rock separates the upper field from a long lower bowl. We take a moment to chart a course, looking for a continuous line of snow that can get us through the rocks to the lower field. We look for depressions and chutes where the heaviest snow tends to accumulate. We study lateral angles, scanning the terrain for a route that's flat and steep enough to accommodate a long sequence of turns. We want to maximize our chances for a good run. To do this, we have to position ourselves in accordance with the features of the mountain.

And down we go, cutting tracks around the islands of rock, adjusting the angle of turns to the demands of gravity and terrain. Dropping through the maze, we find a balance on the back ski edge, a rhythm through the rocks, following the lines and curves of the mountain until we break out of the glade onto a long half-mile run down to tundra. Beyond the north rim, Quandary drops a thousand feet into a chasm. I pick a route not far from the edge and ski on, carving grooves in the summer snow, feeling the presence of the *void* close by. The snow is softer here, more consistent. Along the edge of the precipice, I lock into a lulling rhythm of turn after turn after telemark turn, and for a moment I lose myself in a feeling just beyond conscious thought.

Maybe Proust could appreciate this, after all. If not the spirit of backcountry skiing, then perhaps the duality of perception implicit in its story—however conscious the story finally is in the end. For Proust, remembrance was every-thing. It was both the driving force behind his work and the very means by which one could transcend the inexorable march of time toward death. To re-capture past time, to relive past impressions in those profoundly autonomous moments when the past overwhelms the present, was for him a triumph over time itself. Destiny derailed, if you will. Think of it. Two selves ponder the same event: one on the mountain looking to lose a little something of himself in the technique of telemark skiing, the other reflecting back on it. One expe-riencing, the other *re*-experiencing. And in the act of narration the selves inter-sect, become simultaneous in a common essence distilled from the processes of language, what amounts to a purely essentialist view of things.

But you can't stretch time without a mountain, and there's no story with-out snow. Finding a rhythm in its contours and conditions, we participate in the beauty and logic of a mountain. Consciousness passes somewhere in be-tween, and forgetting becomes its own form of remembrance. In our *relation* to the rock, we're reminded of our vital connection to the earth, our humble origins in the primordial ooze. Through technique and form we recall the changes and transitions of nature, fall in step with the whirl of earth and sea-son, sun and moon...all turning to the steady rhythm of creation time. We came out of a mountain, after all. Why shouldn't we think like one?

The last descent is a good thirty-five yards wide. Chance and I run it side by side in loose telemark choreography, finding the right serpentine pattern in the soft contours of Quandary. I can see him out of the corner of my eye, rising and falling with each arc and glide of turn. I go until my thighs scream agony and I just can't muscle another turn, dropping in the snow to gaze up at the long, slow march of summer clouds in the sky. Sun and ice strike an agreeable balance somewhere along the spine, as the pain in my legs mounts and recedes in a wave of euphoric oxygen. Not a ski's length away, the petals and pinnate lobes of an alpine aven shine in the sun at the edge of the snow-field. Would the flower look as precious, I wonder, if not for the ice? The ice as lovely, if not for the flower? Looking up at the clouds I realize I could be al-most anywhere, and it occurs to me that there is nothing unlikely about these mountains at all.

We step off the snowfield into moss campion, Rocky Mountain nail-wort, and a showy tableau of summer—careful to use the rocks when we can.

Snowmelt purls under the tundra cushion, and we follow it down to a pool where we help ourselves to a handful of sweet mountain runoff. Behind us, our two sets of tracks wind thirty turns up the glaring snowfield as we take a minute to study them, looking critically for any hitch in delivery. Tracks don't lie. As definite and precise as the tracks look now, they too are destined for the sun and wind, the snow and rain.

Back to the trail again and across the talus we go: glissading down patches of wet snow from terrace to lower terrace. The wind rises up and starts the flowers in a wild, ecstatic quiver. King's crown, kittentails, chiming bells, and clover... all wired, it seems, into some crazy triple-time jig. And lookee there. If it isn't the blazing countenance of Old Man of the Mountains, rare native resident of the high Rockies.

The solstice sun sits on the edge of the mountain as we descend into the warm space of scattered evergreens. Looking up I see Chance, ski poles in hand, bounding down the trail through the grinning slice of shadow and light that splits the air.

But it's hardly me, anymore.

Hardly me on the mountain, but off someplace else: at some distant outpost of time looking back to reimagine myself, a friend, and a mountainside of trembling wildflowers. All lost in a shining radiance of memory.

6.   *We Are Here, Who Are You?*

A trail courses through cactus and sage, staying close along the rim of Bullet Canyon. Blue flax and globe mallow bend in the wind that sweeps across the mesa on this clear spring day. From the shade of a juniper tree, we peer down into a jumbled landscape of boulders and slabs, walls and ledges, bunchgrass and shrubs. All of it harsh in the glare of a high sun.

We start down where the trail drops over the rim, squeezing between sandstone blocks, edging across slickrock to the sandy wash below. Walking west through the dappled shade of cottonwoods, we drop deeper into the canyon with each step. There's a different feeling now that we're inside the canyon. The landscape seems less imposing, more intimate. The canyon walls enclose us in endless nuances of eroded stone—undercuts, ledges, overhangs, bedrock. Hard country to be sure, but beautiful in its austerity.

Bullet Canyon is part of a labyrinth of drainages, stretching from Red House Cliffs in the west to Cedar Mesa in the east. This network of canyons and gulches drains the mesas and ridges of Grand Gulch Plateau, emptying into the San Juan River that then joins the Colorado River, all tending in a southwesterly direction for the Baja delta. The Henrys to the northwest, the La Sals to the northeast, we make our way deeper into the Four Corners backcountry.

Home of the Anasazi.

For thousands of years, ancient southwestern peoples inhabited the canyons and mesas of the Colorado Plateau. First living in nomadic hunting-and-gathering societies, these ancestral Puebloans gradually developed an agrarian way of life with the arrival of domesticated corn from the south. The transformation to a more sedentary existence gave rise to a culture we know today as the Anasazi. Over time, villages appeared and large housing structures were built. Through a far-reaching system of trade and ritual, the Anasazi developed a society consisting of as many as twenty thousand farmsteads. But then it all changed. Coinciding with two major droughts in the late eleventh and early twelfth centuries, the people abandoned their farms and society, migrating first to the uplands and later to riverine locations mainly in the Rio Grande drainage. By 1300, for reasons that are still not entirely clear, the Anasazi had deserted the Four Corners region altogether.

Today, Anasazi ruins lie scattered across the southern Colorado Plateau and upper Rio Grande region, an area extending over one hundred thousand square miles. Evidence of this ancient culture survives in the remains of masonry dwellings, granaries and kivas, pottery shards, tools, pictographs and petroglyphs. Many of these dwellings look as if they were abandoned only yesterday, the artifacts of everyday life left behind in their familiar places. It may be centuries since they were last here, but their presence is clearly felt.

Mo and I continue down the bedrock wash, following the contours of the drainage as it winds past deep undercuts and weatherworn boulders. Tall and athletic, my friend cuts a striking figure on the trail. Of biracial ancestry, Mo was raised in South Dakota by her grandfather, a traditional Lakota elder. A former student of mine, now in graduate school for American Indian studies, she's agreed to accompany me for four days in Grand Gulch, an area known for its many ruins. I've asked her along to share her insights and help me better understand the Anasazi experience. The original human adventure in the place I call home.

We are well into afternoon, now. A serrated shadow of rimrock stretches across the wash. White clouds drift in a dome of blue sky. At one point, the trail leaves the wash and climbs the side of the canyon before cresting a ridge and dropping into a spacious park. With the sun directly before us, we walk into a field of backlit wildflowers: orange globe mallow, white evening primrose, red penstemon, purple lupine. Among such resplendent color, we keep on through the meadow of light. I pinch a sprig of sage between my fingers, inhaling the scent for sustenance.

A few miles before the confluence with Grand Gulch, our destination for the night, we scramble up a steep slope to reach Perfect Kiva, a ruin situated high along a ledge beneath a cliff overhang. A stone-and-mortar dwelling sits behind the kiva, its ceiling constructed with wooden crossbeams and mud. Not far away, four cylindrical grooves are worn into a large rock. This metate is where corn was ground, with a round stone called a mano. The meal was likely passed from groove to groove where it could be worked into a finer form, then patted into cakes and cooked before an open fire. I run my finger inside one of the grooves, feeling the fine layer of dust.

As the largest structure in the alcove, the kiva occupies a prominent place. Modeled after the pit houses of early Anasazi society, kivas likely served as gathering places for families and clans. As the culture became more sedentary, the kiva was formalized into a ceremonial chamber. This is where people gathered for ritual observations and important ceremonies.

Judging from all the footprints outside, Perfect Kiva has seen many visitors. I grab hold of the pinyon ladder extending from the opening of the kiva and start down, noticing the shiny new bolts at each rung. No doubt, this ruin is carefully watched and maintained. Feeling a bit like a tourist, I descend into the kiva where it's nice and cool inside, a welcome relief from the sun and heat. The round chamber is fully enclosed by rock and mortar walls, a mud-and-beam ceiling, and a dirt floor where I take a seat. A subtle aroma of fire smoke pervades the room. Overhead, the square entrance lets in a soft light. There's a feeling of stillness here, of sanctuary.

I try to imagine the people who used this room centuries ago. I imagine them here in the chamber, with smoke and song and a square of sky at the top of the ladder. A fire burns low in the pit. Dust particles drift through a bar of light. A family gathers. Old men tell stories.

But then something happens. The Native theme song from a television documentary enters my head. Photographs of famous Indians flash through my mind—Geronimo, Sitting Bull, Red Cloud. It's as if I'm unable to get beyond this facade of popular images, this screen of icons. Suddenly, it feels all wrong. Part of the reason for visiting these ruins is to try to see the world from a different perspective. But if this is as far as my perception goes, then maybe I have no business being here.

And yet it feels good to be in the kiva. The feeling of stillness remains. Relax, I tell myself. Take a deep breath.

If there was a fire pit and deflector in Perfect Kiva, they are no longer visible. Neither is there evidence of a *sipapu*—the small hole, or "earth navel," along the floor that signifies the point of human emergence. This is where people entered into the light of the Fourth World from the dark world of chaos below. According to Hopi story, Tawa the Creator devised an order of peace and harmony and created the First World for people to comprehend the meaning of things. But when they began fighting, Tawa destroyed the First World by fire. Only those who remembered the Creator's plan were saved from the destruction. The Second World was created before it too was destroyed when people became full of greed and made war. The pattern repeated itself in the Third World, when people forgot the meaning of life and the world became full of corruption and chaos. "A faithful few remembered," writes Reg Saner in *The Four-Cornered Falcon*. "In their songs they asked, 'Who are we? Where do we come from? Why are we here?' Their answers reminded them: they had been created by Tawa, the sun. They had come through many worlds. Evil in the human heart had brought each to ruin. So they rose into the Fourth World, leaving evil behind."

Outside, through the opening at the top of the ladder, the alcove ceiling glows in reflected sunlight. Clouds sail through a blue sky. Down by the wash, cottonwoods and willow grow along the sandbars. Beyond Grand Gulch, the windswept mesas of juniper and pinyon give way to red-rock canyons and forested mountains. And farther out: cars and roads, highways and interstates, power lines and dams, and all the hell-bent fury of modern society.

I get up to leave. It seems I could stay a while, but dusk approaches. My partner waits. I climb the ladder and reemerge in sunlight.

We make camp that night along a bench above the confluence. High above us, a small ruin overlooks the canyon with two eyelike windows. As darkness falls, Venus rises in the sky amid a graffiti of contrails and blinking lights from jetliners and satellites.

Around midnight, we are visited by the curious inhabitant of a deep recess in the rock. Bobcat, maybe, who keeps a safe distance on the periphery.

*   *   *

In the morning, we start down Grand Gulch to see what we can find in the way of ruins and water. The standing water at the confluence looks bad—stagnant pools choked with mosquito larvae and other debris. Before leaving the confluence, we look behind us and mark the position of the two-eyed dwelling above our camp.

We follow the trail west, past sandbars etched with the footprints of great blue heron. A flock of mourning doves takes flight, the whir of wings rising in the air. A gust of wind starts a flurry of cottonwood seeds.

On we go through thickets of sage and tamarisk, at times so high their limbs arch over the trail. Walking through a plain of cheatgrass, thick up to the thigh, I lose my bearings. It seems I'm standing still, and the grass is rushing past in a flood of sea foam.

Cheatgrass, like tamarisk, is an exotic species. Introduced to the West in the late 1800s, it established itself in areas damaged by overgrazing and cultivation, outcompeting native grasses and "cheating" farmers of their crop. Tamarisk, on the other hand, was introduced from the Middle East in the early 1800s to control erosion along rivers and streambeds. Arriving in Utah sometime around 1880, wild tamarisk quickly asserted its dominance over native willows and cottonwoods along river corridors. As invasive species, both cheatgrass and tamarisk have dramatically altered the canyon ecosystems of southern Utah.

This is, in many respects, a different place from what the ancients saw. Although it remains uncertain when humans first arrived to the Four Corners region, archaeological evidence suggests that small bands of Paleo-Indians were living in the Southwest twelve thousand years ago and probably much earlier. These early people were hunters and gatherers, following herds of mammoths and huge bison and other megafauna of the Pleistocene. They hunted with Clovis-style projectile points, often trapping and killing entire herds. The big herds were supported by a lush grassland ecosystem that flourished in the wet and cool climate of the late Ice Age. For five thousand years or so, Paleo-Indians led a nomadic way of life, subsisting primarily on the meat of big game in addition to what they could find in the way of edible plants.

By the end of the Pleistocene, the large herds of game had vanished. While overhunting may have contributed to the extinction of some megafauna during the late Ice Age, it's important to remember that a rapid and dramatic change in climate occurred at this time. After 5000 BC, the Southwest became significantly warmer and drier, even more than what exists today. Paleoclimatologists refer to this event as the Altithermal. During this period, southwestern peoples came to rely more on the gathering of edible plants such as yucca, prickly pear, pinyon, sego lily, wild onions, and Indian ricegrass. They hunted small game to supplement their primary dependency on plants. Living a seminomadic existence, these Desert Archaic people traveled in extended families and small bands, taking shelter in caves and rock overhangs along canyon walls. They limited their possessions—tools, baskets, nets, snares, stone points—to what they could carry with them, as they made their seasonal rounds according to the movement of game and the ripening of wild plants.

By 3000 BC or so, the climate turned cooler and wetter. As grasslands became more abundant, animals such as deer, elk, bison, and bighorn sheep moved into the region. The return of big game resulted in a steady increase in population. Any pressures caused by growing numbers of people would ultimately be alleviated by a greater dependence on corn. Although it would be centuries before ancient peoples embraced agriculture as a way of life in the Four Corners region, it would transform the culture profoundly and give rise to the people known as the Anasazi.

"We have to be careful with our language," Mo says as we hike along the wash. Walking ahead of me, she turns to speak over her shoulder. "A western perspective is going to reflect an historical bias. It's also going to privilege technology. So, when we use words like 'developed' and 'advanced' to describe societies, we're really imposing a cultural bias that assumes that all cultures exist on a track of development toward some higher point, namely, modern industrial society. Thus, we tend to think of a 'hunter-gatherer' society as a primitive stage of human culture. We tend to think of it as inferior to agrarian societies that rely more on technology."

Her point about language reminds me that the name "Anasazi" is really a Navajo word that translates into "enemies of our ancestors," reflecting the animosity that once existed between local Navajo bands and Puebloan farming villages. Understandably, contemporary Pueblo Indians reject the term "Anasazi" as it is used to describe their ancestors, preferring instead "the ancient ones."

"People will make logical choices based on what they are presented with," Mo continues, "even as they interpret what they're presented with differently. It seems to me these early people were making commonsense choices. What we call 'hunting and gathering' made perfect sense given the conditions of the land. After all, why settle down when there is such a plentiful food source in wild plants and migrating herds of animals? People chose a nomadic way of life because it fit the rhythms of the land."

After four miles of hiking, we come upon a ruin near the entrance to Step Canyon. The ruin is situated along an alcove 150 feet above the canyon floor. After some careful navigation, we reach the ledge and the remains of a dwelling.

Narrow in places, the alcove is long enough to accommodate a number of structures. At one end, a two-story apartment extends nearly to the edge of the cliff. The two levels are separated by a mud-and-beam partition that serves as both floor and ceiling. Both rooms have windows that overlook the canyon. A second rock-and-mortar structure occupies the opposite end of the alcove in the shadow of the overhang. On the wall behind it is a pictograph of a human form with a triangular torso and head. There are other apartments in the alcove, as well as scattered ears of corn, potsherds, and fragments of chert. The pottery sherds appear in both coiled and flat styles. Much of the pottery here is highly decorated. Like so many of the ruins in Grand Gulch, this dwelling contains artifacts from different periods.

Archaeologists tend to distinguish different stages of Anasazi culture according to a system known as the Pecos Classification. Divided into two main groups, this system comprises eight stages in all. The Basketmaker stages (I–III) are located historically between 200 BC to AD 700, whereas the Pueblo stages (I–V) extend from AD 700 to the present. The two groups are distinguished by the use of baskets, on one hand, and the subsequent use of pottery as the culture transformed into an agrarian way of life revolving around permanent settlements.

Although it's not clear exactly when domesticated corn arrived here, archaeological evidence suggests that it was being cultivated in the Four Corners region by 1500 BC. Indian corn, or maize, is native to the Western Hemisphere and adapts well to the kind of dry climates experienced in the semiarid Southwest. A source of vitamins, minerals, fats, and carbohydrates, maize offered the nutritional equivalent of many wild plants gathered over a large area. It dried well and could be stored for those times when food was scarce.

Initially, maize played only a minor role in the diet of Archaic peoples who still depended upon traditional foraging. A favorable climate may have allowed people to maintain their traditional hunter-gatherer way of life while exploring the possibilities of horticulture by experimenting with various strategies and techniques. By 500 BC, some groups had developed large-cobbed varieties of corn that could grow under various conditions and produce bigger yields. Squash was also being cultivated at this time. With the introduction of beans, the nutritional benefits of farming increased significantly. While corn has substantial nutritional value, it lacks some of the amino acids necessary to make complete protein. Beans, on the other hand, contain lysine—an important amino acid in the making of protein. Thus, a balanced diet of corn, squash, and beans could provide the complementary amino acids to meet many of their nutritional needs.

Beginning around 500 BC, the region experienced longer periods of drought, prompting late Archaic people to intensify their agricultural efforts. In drought conditions, the cultivation of corn and beans and squash proved to be a more reliable method of producing food than traditional foraging. With a slightly more reliable food supply, people were apt to be less nomadic as they tended their crops. Although formal agriculture was not yet practiced, the way of life gradually became more sedentary. Campsites became larger and more permanent. Storage pits were dug to stockpile the harvest.

As people in the Southwest became more stationary, different cultural groups began to develop: the Anasazi in the Four Corners region, the Mogollon in what is today eastern Arizona and southwestern New Mexico, the Hohokam in the Sonoran Desert, the Sinagua in central Arizona, and the Salado in southern Arizona. These groups continued to interact with each other, trading goods and exchanging information.

Archaeologists locate the emergence of Anasazi culture sometime around 200 BC. The early Anasazi are remembered for their tightly woven baskets made from both coiled and plaited plant fibers. The baskets were used to prepare meals, transport water, and store grain. As their way of life became more sedentary, these early Basketmakers began a transition from rock shelters to partially underground pit houses—walled structures of wood-and-mud masonry. If only on a seasonal basis, they lived in small villages where they developed greater storage capacities for their crops. By this time, the Basketmakers had experimented with and developed specific strains of corn and beans. They ground their corn into meal at basin metates with one-hand manos. Stone axes were developed to cut logs for the pit houses. It was about this time, too, that the bow and arrow were introduced from tribes of the northern plains. For clothing, the early Basketmakers made loincloths, string aprons, and robes from turkey feathers and animal furs. They wove sandals from the fiber of yucca and other plants.

By AD 500, the Basketmakers were living in villages consisting of fifty pit houses, with greater and more elaborate storage facilities. Though the size of the pit houses became smaller in these larger villages, their construction improved: excavated walls were lined with stone slabs or mud plaster, roofs were supported by four posts, floor plans became more sophisticated. Some of these pit houses included central fire pits, deflectors, and sipapus.

The Anasazi also began to make pottery. Introduced from the south, perhaps from villagers in the Mogollan Mountains, utilitarian pottery eventually replaced basketry for many everyday functions. Among other things, pottery allowed the Anasazi to be more efficient in cooking. As different shapes and decorative styles developed, pottery became an important commodity for trade. By now, the Anasazi trading range extended from the Gulf of Mexico to the Gulf of California.

As of AD 700, the Anasazi were building aboveground housing blocks, or pueblos. It was about this time that the community house emerged as an important gathering place for people. Round in design and typically larger than other pit-house structures, the community house would eventually evolve into the ceremonial chamber, or kiva. The Anasazi developed new rituals and ceremonies to reflect their transformation to an agrarian way of life. There were changes in social organization as well. Population expanded considerably during this period, as evidenced by the increase in artifacts and storage structures.

"It was a time of dramatic change," Mo says beside the two-story structure, pieces of red and black chert scattered at her feet. "I imagine it was a difficult way of life, but in many respects, a rich and fulfilling one too."

From the alcove, we enjoy a wide view of the canyon. The leaves of tall cottonwoods, bright green in sunlight, flutter in the breeze. Their shadows flicker across the white sand along the wash.

"Certainly, there was a lot of work involved—planting and tending crops, grinding seed, making pottery and tools and clothes, building and repairing structures. With an increase in agriculture, there's going to be specialization of labor. Anthropologists will tell you to expect a greater attention to spiritual matters as well, the assumption being that a more complex social organization allows time for people to develop more sophisticated rituals and ceremonies. On the other hand, the increased use of land may have caused people to be wary. By putting more demands on the land through agriculture, people may have felt they needed to depend more on the benevolence of spirits."

We linger a while on the ledge. Mo sits with her back against the rock, her long straight hair falling nearly to her waist. Her speech is measured, the words chosen carefully. Although she thinks primarily in English, she says there are times when she thinks in Lakota first and then translates that understanding into English. This is particularly true when the ideas and meanings become more complex.

"Living so close to the rhythms of nature, I imagine every task had a purpose. Everything had a cosmological significance, a place in the grand scheme of things. Animals, plants, family obligations, kinship ties, work…It all added up to a purposeful way of life."

On our way back to camp, we stop beside a pool of water to fill the bottles. Filtering water is a tedious process. As our feet sink into the quicksand at the edge of the pool, flycatchers whir overhead, darting above the tamarisk. Back on the trail we lock into a hiking rhythm, following the path as it crisscrosses the wash. Finally, coming around a corner, we see the two-eyed dwelling high on the canyon wall.

Home.

As darkness falls, we cook dinner over a gas burner and make tea. A bat flutters overhead. Western pipistrelle, if I had to guess.

Something moves along the rock ledge, on the periphery where light dissolves to dark. Our friend the cat, most likely. Who, perhaps, may be anxious on account of spring kittens in her nearby den.

My partner reassures the animal in soft tones. No harm intended, she imparts. Apologies for the infringement.

Later, in the wee hours of the night, the cat investigates our camp, purring as it makes its rounds.

In the morning, we hike off the bench and pick up the hardpan trail leading north into Grand Gulch. Two hours after sunup, and it's already scorching hot.

At the junction with Sheik Canyon, we stow the packs and start up the sandy wash, carrying bags and bottles in hopes of finding good water along Green Mask Spring. Past the ruin, the spring collects in shallow basins of bedrock. The higher we go, the better the water. We hike to the highest pool, where we begin the painstaking process of filling each bottle and bag under a blazing sun, all the while observing the antics of tadpoles and snails and backswimmers. There are tiny shrimp, too. A caddis fly larva skirts the bottom of the pool, dragging its cumbersome casing. A blue dragonfly touches down on the packed mud.

Back at the ruin, we climb to the rock ledge where we find a kiva and an impressive panel of rock art. The kiva is without a roof, and sand fills much of the subterranean chamber. The design is more elaborate than what we saw at Perfect Kiva. Sitting benches line the base of the walls. Two spiral designs are etched along the back wall; one has nine rings in the spiral, the other seven. The rings might indicate the number of years the ledge was inhabited before it was abandoned—a chronicle of migration left behind for others to see. We were here, now we are gone.

On the wall above the ledge, red and gray pictographs cover the rock: handprints, snakes, and large triangular human figures. There are a number of vertical lines with circles at the top, indicating pools of water perhaps. The torsos of two headless anthropomorphs are decorated with dots, each with four blank rectangles in the upper-chest area. It could be these life-size human figures were painted to allow the spirits of deceased warriors or shamans to come and go from the rock as they pleased.

But there is something I missed, something that only now emerges on the wall. Behind the boldly stroked pictographs, I begin to see faint images of human bodies with elaborate, birdlike heads. It seems the pictographs have been superimposed upon petroglyphs. And what does this mean?

There are other pictographs to contemplate on the wall, more abstract in design: trapezoids with squiggly horizontal lines, a cluster of what appear to be heron tracks, a sequence of vertical lines, something that looks like a gliding raptor. But who's to say?

At various times, the prehistoric rock art of southwestern peoples seems to describe events, geographic features, wildlife, the stars, visions and dreams. In our art today, we allow for ambiguity and the possibility of multiple meanings. Why shouldn't we accord the same latitude to these artists, especially in light of a worldview that emphasizes interrelations? Whatever the meanings here, one thing is clear: the images resonate with energy. Voice and vision speak across the centuries.

The ruins at Sheik Canyon indicate a Puebloan presence. Like their ancestors, early Puebloans adopted change in deliberate fashion, incorporating new ways of doing things over the course of time. And while the rate of change may have varied across the region, the culture overall became increasingly agrarian. The Anasazi grew more proficient as farmers, terracing and irrigating their fields. They began to cultivate cotton, finding it more effective than plant fiber in the weaving of clothes. Individual villages developed their own polychrome styles of pottery. Trade increased among communities.

By now, the Anasazi were building larger villages that became increasingly standardized. Storage capacity grew. In these planned villages, pit houses gave way to surface structures, many of which had walls constructed of posts that were then covered with adobe and rock facings. These surface structures, or *jacals*, were used both as residences and as storage areas. The early Puebloans built these jacals in clusters, often in the form of arced rows with a traditional kiva situated in front. Some villages contained a hundred rooms and more than a dozen pit houses, supporting as many as six hundred people. Typically, early Puebloan villages were occupied for only thirty or forty years before they were abandoned.

Mo and I return to our packs along the sandy wash at the mouth of Sheik Canyon. At the junction, we turn north again into Grand Gulch. But it's tough to keep ahead of my thirst in this heat. It seems I'm sucking water too fast. The trail winds along the drainage before veering off into willow and tamarisk, returning to the top of a cutbank, then down into the rocks of the wash, and up again into shrubs where it continues its serpentine course. A mile farther, I get turned around on a sage flat where the canyon opens up and at least three drainages lead into the park. Disoriented, I struggle to find our north-northeasterly direction. We retrace our steps and pick up the trail again with the sun at our backs, watching the topography till it's clear we're on the right path.

We are seeing a lot of ruins now, mostly isolated structures tucked inside the ledges of walls. Some are two hundred feet high above the canyon floor, and almost all face south. From a defensive standpoint, it makes sense that these structures should be where they are. Many of these dwellings could have been reached only with the aid of a ladder or rope dropped from above. If a band of marauding raiders threatened a dwelling and the only means of access was a ladder, why, the ladder could be quickly pulled onto the ledge. With proper vigilance, it seems these dwellings could easily be defended.

We stop for lunch in the shade of a pinyon, dropping our forty-five-pound packs. Surrounded by wildflowers and sage, it feels good to rest. Back muscles relax. Feet and shoulders, too. In a cooling breeze, we eat lunch and gradually regain our strength. Enough to indulge in that most basic of human luxuries—philosophy. I ruminate on the nature of my being: a big bag of fluid in a hot and dry place, entirely dependent upon the water we carry on our backs. Out here, matters are reduced to a basic level. The desert imposes itself in no uncertain terms.

Not surprisingly, the availability of water may have been the key factor in the remarkable rise of Anasazi society. By the late 700s, two distinct patterns of rainfall existed in the Southwest. Chaco Canyon, located in northwestern New Mexico, straddled the boundary between the two regimes. The area to the west and north of Chaco received most of its precipitation during the winter and summer months, while the area to the south and southeast received its precipitation primarily in mid- to late summer. In *Anasazi America*, David Stuart suggests that Chaco became the center of a vast network of trade and distribution by effectively spreading the risks of drought over an entire region. Widespread farming virtually guaranteed that enough localities would receive adequate rainfall to ensure at least a small surplus of harvested crops. The Anasazi expanded existing farms and developed new farming communities where none existed before. Archaeologists estimate that ten thousand farmsteads were established in a 150-year period beginning in the 800s. As the center of storage and trade, Chaco engineered the transfer of surplus crops from those farmsteads that prospered in any given year to those that didn't.

During this time, the Chaco Anasazi built multistoried sites called *great houses* that provided residential, storage, and ritual space. Nine of these large pueblos were built in Chaco Canyon along with hundreds of smaller structures, providing thousands of individual rooms. Pueblo Bonito, one of the more spectacular great houses at Chaco, covered an area of almost five acres. Bonito contained nearly seven hundred rooms, roughly half of which were used for storage. Like other great houses at Chaco, Bonito was built with the cosmos in mind. Windows were designed to accentuate the sun's light at summer solstice. Kivas and plazas were constructed to mark the paths of the sun and moon.

The Chaco system began with the great houses and settlements of Chaco Canyon and radiated out to include a network of farming communities called outliers. The farmsteads, after all, were what supported and maintained the Chaco system. Beginning around 1000, midsummer rains became more predictable, allowing the expansion of farming into new areas. For the most part, this favorable pattern of summer rain continued for the next 130 years, resulting in decades of above-average harvests. As farming expanded and new communities developed, the infrastructure and architecture became more complex. Beginning in earnest around 1050, the Anasazi built a formal road system totaling four hundred miles that connected outlying farming communities with the great houses of Chaco Canyon. The Anasazi also developed a communication system composed of signaling stations built on hilltops. By way of signal fires and reflective slabs of obsidian, the great houses in Chaco Canyon could communicate with the outliers.

Chacoan society reached its zenith in the period between 1020 and 1130, extending throughout the entire San Juan River basin and into the surrounding foothills. With its kivas and great houses, Chaco Canyon stood at the center of this far-reaching system of ritual and trade. Food and seed were stored in the great houses and then traded for pottery, meat, cotton, and other goods. The Chaco system worked as long as there was consistent rainfall and the expanding farmsteads could keep pace with a growing population.

But a prolonged drought in the 1090s, lasting five or six years, changed all that. The drought affected food production and, ultimately, the ability of Chacoan society to feed its large population. Facing malnutrition and starvation, small farmers abandoned the outliers in search of places where they could find water, firewood, and upland game. The Chacoan response to this crisis was to build new roads and increase development, employing many of the displaced farmers. The practice of ritual intensified. When the rains returned, Chacoans redoubled their efforts—building more and greater kivas. Most of the new development occurred in the northern basin. By the early 1100s, the center of Anasazi society had shifted to the north of the San Juan River to such places as Aztec, Escalante, Ida Jean, and Wallace.

One of the remarkable features of Chacoan society was the fact that its residents—many of whom came from different ethnic, tribal, and linguistic backgrounds—lived peacefully in unfortified communities. For centuries, the Anasazi maintained an open society. People moved freely along the roads, with unrestricted access to the kivas and courtyards of the great houses. That all changed in the late 1000s in the wake of the droughts. For the first time, the Chacoan great houses became fortified. Walls were constructed to control access to courtyards, especially those close to roads. Tower kivas were built, presumably as both ceremonial sites and watchtowers.

A second prolonged drought, lasting from about 1135 to 1150, sealed the fate of Chacoan society. Any combination of overpopulation, exhausted resources, or social factionalism may have contributed to its final demise, but it's clear that the Chacoan system simply could not withstand the pressures brought on by an extended drought. By 1140, the Chaco Phenomenon was over. What followed was a period of social upheaval as people scattered throughout the region, migrating mostly to the surrounding uplands where there was greater precipitation and better foraging opportunities in the way of wild plants and game. In a time characterized by chaos and violence, warring factions clashed over what resources the land could provide. The fall of Chacoan society exacted a heavy toll, resulting in a dramatic decline in population. To make matters worse, recent archaeological evidence suggests that

Athabascan peoples—ancestors of the Navajo—may have been migrating into the area as early as the late 1100s. If indeed this is true, their presence would have only exacerbated an already difficult situation for the Anasazi.

Eventually, the violence and chaos subsided to the point that new trading networks developed among the small settlements scattered across the mesas and talus slopes of the uplands. By 1200, people were building large pueblo sites at Mesa Verde, in the Zuni highlands, along the northern Rio Grande, and elsewhere. Distinct from Chacoan great houses, these cliff dwellings—built in alcoves under stone overhangs—were more compact and angular in design. The multistoried masonry pueblos of this period were clearly built with defense in mind. Many could be reached only by way of footholds and handholds pecked into the cliffs.

As precipitation increased and became more predictable, the upland society flourished. People traded pottery again, as this new economy connected communities ranging across an area of sixty thousand square miles. But drought returned to the region in the 1260s, and the Mesa Verde country was soon abandoned. Within a decade, most of the remaining Anasazi pueblos were concentrated in the northern Rio Grande area where people could depend on a reliable water source. The Anasazi deserted their ancestral homelands of the San Juan River basin and the uplands to the north. Shortly after 1300, they were gone from Grand Gulch and the entire Four Corners region.

"When the droughts came, I believe the people thought they were doing something wrong," Mo says as we walk. "The ancestors were upset with them, and the dry years were evidence of that. Obviously, widespread farming is going to have a big impact on the land, especially one as arid as this. I believe people felt that their way of life was out of balance and they needed to change. Rather than relying on technology to mitigate the effects of drought, they made a conscious choice to follow a different path."

On our approach to Split Level, the canyon widens considerably. A high ceiling of clouds eclipses the sun, and the hiking doesn't seem nearly as arduous in the absence of direct sunlight.

"You have to remember that, in this worldview, everything is interconnected and capable of influencing everything else. All things possess spirit and power and exist within a continuum encompassing the totality of time. There is no distinction here between the sacred and secular, earth and religion. Ancestors, spirits, and gods are inextricably tied to everyday activities. What you do to the earth, you do to the ancestors and the children who have yet to be born. People—as well as the plants and animals that sustain us—all exist in the same life cycle that sees one generation to the next. It only makes sense to live in harmony with these rhythms. To be right with family and community, earth and cosmos."

At Split Level, we notice a number of ruins along a spacious alcove 150 feet above the canyon floor. The biggest resembles a garrison—a massive rock-and-mud structure that stands two or three stories high. At least nine beams protrude from the base of its roof. All the ruins here seem virtually inaccessible. Protected from rain and snow and the greedy reach of pottery hunters, Split Level appears to be in pristine condition. Hiking up from the south, I get the distinct impression these dwellings are still inhabited.

We are here, they seem to say. *Who are you?*

Following the winding course of the wash, we make our way through greasewood and sage and prickly pear. We're seeing all kinds of ruins now, mostly small granaries and apartments.

Past Lion Track Springs, we come upon Pour Off Pool—a murky hole of water that looks especially inviting. The temptation is to strip down and cool off, wash the sweat and grime from our bodies. A rocky spigot looms twenty feet above the pool, where floodwater pours when the wash runs high. The spectacle of flash floods is betrayed by eroded grooves in the rock. By stains on the stone.

The sculpted sandstone here reminds us of the geologic forces at work in this part of the West. Grand Gulch is entirely entrenched in a cross-bedded rock unit known as Cedar Mesa Sandstone, a massive formation that covers the Grand Gulch Plateau. This formation was created from the sandbars and drifting beaches of a sea that moved down from the northwest 250 million years ago. As the sea retreated, winds blew the sand into layered deposits that eventually formed the white to reddish brown sandstone. Since then, the forces of erosion have carved canyons and gullies. As the largest of the San Juan tributary canyons, Grand Gulch provided good habitation for ancient peoples in the way of alcoves, overhangs, river bottoms, and springs.

At the junction with Todie Canyon, we enter a burned-out cottonwood stand and the stark beauty of bare trees set against wildflowers and lush grass.

In this skeletal forest, the cottonwood trunks are smooth and ghostly gray. Branches are craggy and charred. The scene looks remotely Gothic, as if the forest were inhabited by spirits of the dead—ancient ones watching over their ground.

We stay to the north through the junction as daylight begins to fade. A few miles past Todie, we settle on a campsite beneath a juniper tree near Turkey Pen Ruin. Archaeologists believe people inhabited this site, perhaps continually, from the time of Basketmaker II through Pueblo III—a period of a thousand years or so. The ruin was looted sometime around 1979, denying archaeologists what might have been an unprecedented look at Anasazi life. At the back of the alcove, near the remains of a rock-and-mortar structure, two white pictographs are painted in the shape of birds. Soot blackens the back wall, except for borders of clean rock where the structure once stood. These "ghost walls" indicate where adjacent apartments were separated before the structure collapsed. There are white handprints, too, and a pictograph in the shape of a human.

Once again, I feel the presence of ancient people. In the stillness of dusk I can almost hear the soft laughter of women grinding seed against stone, see a film of camp smoke in the canyon air, feel the heft of a stone pipe as the first stars appear in the sky.

We organize the gear and tally the last of the food. On the blue flame of the burner, we cook a freeze-dried concoction and eat dinner on ground where the ancients once walked. Seated at the base of the canyon wall, not far from the ruin, I can't shake the nagging suspicion that we're being watched.

"It's not surprising," Mo says, her back against the juniper tree. "Ruins are sacred. Spirits inhabit these places, and they command respect."

To this day, Puebloan Indians are reluctant to disturb ancient ruins. There are Pueblo IV riverine sites situated on land held by Puebloans that have never been excavated using modern techniques. It stands to reason that many ruins on Indian lands have never even been reported.

"The spirits are there for people who remain in their home place, the place of their ancestors. Creation stories say people are created for *that* specific place. It is sacred. When a person moves away, the voice is diminished. The relation is more difficult to maintain."

Unlike many Native peoples, Pueblo Indians have remained on the land of their ancestors despite a history of invasion from outside groups. This is probably why Puebloans have been able to preserve their traditional ways more successfully than most. Their experience with different social structures notwithstanding, southwestern peoples have maintained a cultural continuity that goes back to time immemorial. Even the migration of the late 1200s represents just another instance in which ancestral Puebloans transformed themselves to adapt to changing conditions. During the Pueblo IV period, the Anasazi abandoned the Four Corners region in favor of uninhabited farmlands along rivers where they could be assured of a dependable water source. From Taos south along the Rio Grande, and west to the Zuni and Hopi mesas, ancestral Puebloans built new villages and developed a different kind of community.

The villages were located in places where people had access to a variety of ecological zones. By the end of the 1300s, a typical pueblo land might extend from a river to the adjacent foothills and mountains beyond. Through farming and hunting and ritual, each village sought to maintain access to these different zones. The lowlands offered farming opportunities, while the uplands provided access to a variety of large and small game. During summer, villagers might spread out across thirty square miles to farm the pueblo lands, before returning to the village in winter where together they could defend the stored harvest from nomadic raiders. Living along narrow riverine corridors in consolidated villages served a defensive purpose as well.

The people of these Pueblo IV villages utilized diverse and complex strategies in their efforts to build a sustainable and self-sufficient way of life. In addition to the benefits derived from holding diverse lands, Puebloan farmers developed a range of agricultural techniques that allowed them to grow different kinds of corn, beans, squash, and gourds. They pursued multicrop strategies that made them less vulnerable in times of scarcity. In terms of nutrition, the combination of farming and foraging provided a complete diet. Hunting supplied the needed fat and protein, while farming provided fiber and carbohydrates. The Puebloans became extraordinary artisans during this time, producing an array of high-quality goods such as woven cotton, pottery, and jewelry.

Puebloan villagers maintained many of the traditions of their Chacoan ancestors, even as they reshaped them into new forms. Harvests were shared throughout the community. Few pueblos were fortified even though parties of Navajos and Apaches continued to raid, especially in bad years. Puebloans developed an egalitarian and unified social order. Each community shared the same language, customs, and rituals. Members were bound by their obligations to kin and community. In short, Puebloans adapted and innovated as they pursued a way of life designed for stability and long-term survival.

Sunrise.

After a quick meal, we pack up and make the easy one-mile hike to Junction Ruin. This settlement, consisting of twenty structures or so, was used for centuries by ancient peoples. Although a few families may have gathered here at certain times of year during the Basketmaker period, the site was probably not permanently settled until the Pueblo era. Even then, there were likely no more than a few extended families living here at any one time. At the junction of Grand Gulch and Kane Gulch, the site provides an access route to the uplands of Cedar Mesa. With a nearby spring, spacious river bottom, and south-facing alcove, it's a logical choice for a home.

There are two levels of dwellings here: an upper level two hundred feet above the canyon floor where a number of well-preserved structures are tucked inside an alcove, and a lower level near the bottom that is easily accessible. At this lower level we find an array of pit houses and masonry-walled dwellings. Ghost walls shadow the sandstone behind the structures. Corncobs and potsherds, some dating back to Basketmaker times, litter the ground near a mano and metate. In one dwelling, windows offer views both upcanyon and downcanyon—a good way to see who's coming or going. One apartment remains in perfect shape, probably not much different than it looked a thousand years ago.

A large, open kiva is prominently placed along the ledge. As far as I can tell, it's the only circular structure here. All the rest, their walls and windows and doorways, are angular. The circular design speaks to the worldview—the continuum of knowledge, time, and cosmos. This kiva is larger and far more elaborate than any we've seen, with plastered benches and walls and square pillars supporting crossbeams. The bench seating extends around the entire circumference, except for two seats near the hearth. The kiva no longer holds its roof, but when it did, it would have been quite dark inside. One might not have been able to see others seated around the fire. In some kivas, secret passageways were built, presumably where *katsinas* made their dramatic entrances during ceremonies.

Katsinas are the spirits of dead ancestors who return to the world in the form of clouds. Traditional Hopis believe that when a person dies, his spirit or "breath" travels to the underworld where he can assume the characteristics of katsinas. Thus, as part of the burial ritual, a white cotton "cloud mask" is placed upon the face of the deceased. As cloud people, katsinas bring the gift of rain to the Hopi who depend upon corn and other crops for their life. Rain is considered to be the manifestation of the spiritual essence, or *navala*, of katsinas. This underscores the interrelationship of life and death in traditional worldview. In fact, life and death are thought of as mirror images. Insofar as the deceased become katsinas who return to the world and bring rain, death is merely a transition from one stage to another—a necessary phase in a recurrent cycle.

Through ritual and ceremony, the people petition katsinas to send rain so that all things in this world may grow. Prayer offerings are presented in the hope and expectation that they will be answered by the gods and katsinas. This principle of reciprocity is central to Hopi belief. Together with the earth, rainfall is transformed into the corn that feeds the people. In this way, the blessings of the katsinas become the essence of the living human body. Their navala becomes the navala of people. Thus, by way of an essential consubstantiality, cloud masks are related to clouds. The living are connected to the dead.

When the Spanish arrived to the Southwest in 1540, there were somewhere between one and two hundred large pueblos in the region. Most of these—especially those along the arc extending from the Hopi mesas to Zuni and Acoma and north along the Rio Grande—were populated primarily by descendants of the Anasazi. From the beginning, Francisco Vásquez de Coronado and his fellow Spaniards showed little tolerance for the ways of the people they found there. As Christians, the Spanish colonists set out to eradicate the ceremonial practices of the Puebloans. But the people resisted the religious conversion demanded of them by the Spanish. The Puebloans eventually revolted in 1680, driving the Spanish out of New Mexico for the next twelve years. All the while, the population of Puebloan people declined sharply—somewhere on the order of 89 to 95 percent. In spite of such catastrophic losses, the pueblos were able to survive.

Today, a number of Puebloan villages represent the oldest continuously inhabited settlements on the North American continent. Despite nearly five hundred years of outside pressure—first from the Spanish, then the Mexicans, and now the Americans—Puebloan Indians have been able to maintain a semblance of their traditional culture, even as villages have adapted in their own unique ways to the surrounding world. By observing their native language, oral traditions, rituals, and ceremonies, Puebloans have preserved a knowledge base that allows a traditional way of life to endure. Agricultural practices, social customs, economic relations, healing traditions, spiritual matters...all are encoded and transmitted from generation to generation through story and ceremony. The fact that Puebloans have been able to maintain a cultural continuity that goes back thousands of years, despite all the hardships and pressures imposed by outside groups, is testament to their resilience and faith.

It's early in the day, so we're in no hurry. Mo kneels at the edge of the kiva, studying its design, obviously deep in thought. It could be she's contemplating the ceremonial life of Puebloans, or imagining the ancients gathered together in prayer before a fire. Maybe she's thinking about her own people, I don't know. Whatever her reflections, they're bound to be complex. And if that's the case, she's thinking in her native language—thoughts and perceptions that in all likelihood lie somewhere beyond the reaches of my understanding.

I gaze across the bottomland park where the drainages of Kane Gulch and Grand Gulch come together. A breeze rustles the tall cottonwoods growing beside the confluence where the two washes join. Their leaves shimmer in sunlight, as I'm left to ponder a different kind of confluence. Namely, my relation to the ancients. The first people to live in the land that I have come to know and love.

From the edge of the ruin, it occurs to me how much of all this remains beyond my grasp. For days I've tried to see the world from another perspective, but despite my best efforts, all I've been able to glean are brief glimpses of a worldview so different from my own that I hardly know where to begin. No matter how much I'm able to process intellectually, it seems I lack the spiritual wherewithal to take the next step. But even this is a guess. Given all the magnificent ruins scattered about this glorious canyon country, it's no wonder I should take an interest in the Anasazi. And it's not surprising either that the fascination should go beyond a merely historical curiosity to include matters of worldview and way of life—especially those fashioned in the exigencies of the place I call home. Particularly when they make sense.

But I'm no Indian. To presume in any shape or form that I am is pernicious folly.

Yet, after days of exploring these canyons, there is one thread that seems to run through this entire story: the question of how to live according to the terms of the land. For ancestral Puebloans, this meant a collective sustainability in a semiarid region prone to climatic fluctuation and extended periods of drought. For thousands of years, Paleo-Indians led a nomadic life following the big herds of mammoths, huge bison, and other megafauna. When the herds vanished at the close of the Pleistocene, Desert Archaic peoples adopted a more seminomadic existence, relying mainly on the gathering of edible plants. Eventually, Archaic peoples would experiment with agriculture, understanding that the cultivation of maize and other crops provided a more reliable way of producing food in drought conditions. Beginning sometime around AD 800, Anasazi farmers embarked on a strategy that effectively spread the risks of drought over an entire region, combining their efforts to form what many consider to be the greatest prehistoric society in North America. Chacoan society lasted for two hundred years before collapsing in dramatic fashion following a series of regional droughts, prompting the Anasazi to transform themselves yet again, this time into an upland society before it too was abandoned in favor of smaller villages along river corridors where a new kind of community emerged—more modest in scale, certainly, but better equipped for long-term survival. Throughout time, indigenous peoples of the Southwest experimented with different survival strategies in the face of changing conditions and pressures, only to arrive finally at the modest and efficient villages we find today in the pueblos. Place your trust in nature, the experience seems to teach. For this is where we come from, who we are, what sustains us.

From a Puebloan perspective, the modern American way of life must surely look out of balance. It doesn't take much, after all, to see the wasteful ways of our lifestyle. Given the myriad environmental problems that beset the planet—overpopulation, perforated ecosystems, mass extinction, climate change, to name a few—our consumptive habits must seem dangerously out of step. As we continue down a path that threatens the foundations of our sustainability, it must look as though we are ill-prepared to meet the catastrophes that by now seem imminent. Pinning our hopes on a quick technological fix must appear equally as perplexing. With our inefficiency and waste, our infatuation with military power and economic growth, our fragmented attitude toward nature, and our breathtaking reluctance to address the issues in any meaningful way, it all must seem deeply portentous.

I look across the park toward the confluence, taking in the full sweep of the canyon. A raven calls from the cottonwoods. A plume of cumulus sails above rimrock. A whiptail skitters through the ruin, leaving a trail of glyphs in the dust.

Soon, we'll follow the trail up Kane Gulch on our way out of the canyons, passing spectacular slickrock formations and sand-bottom pools the color of copper. We'll pause below stone walls, stained in desert varnish and the long veils of ephemeral waterfalls. Scrambling across sloped and canted bedrock, squeezing through narrow slots, we'll cross the upper reaches of the gulch into scrub oak and box elder, aspen and serviceberry, pinyon pine and Utah juniper. All the while, walking in the footsteps of the ancients.

Once, the greed of man brought chaos to the world. And the people asked: Who are we? Where do we come from? Why are we here?

7. *Greenbacks*

Fern Lake (9,500'), Mid-June

Weather gathers over the Divide, large gray cumulus clouds boiling off the high peaks. Peals of thunder echo through the valleys in the distance. This is where I'm going, I think to myself, stashing the last of the gear into my backpack. Down below on the arid plains, a rust-colored haze spreads east to the horizon. Where I've been.

I follow the trail along Big Thompson Creek, passing a first wave of blooming wildflowers: pink geranium, wild rose, low sunflower. Chiming bells and harebells grow in the shade beside the fast-moving stream. A fragrance of pitch is sharp in the air where the path winds around giant ponderosas and red-rock boulders the size of bungalows. Higher up, a change in vegetation signals the slight transition to cooler climes. Lupine, purple aster, Indian paintbrush. Douglas fir and aspen mix with ponderosa. The trail leaves the Big Thompson for good to begin the long ascent up Fern Creek drainage, where a large admiral butterfly roosts near a patch of purple columbine. I stay longer than I should, watching the slow, rhythmic pulse of black and white wings expanding and contracting.

At the falls, a cool breeze rises off the creek where it tumbles and plunges over deadfall and boulders. Arrow-straight fir trees grow along the edge of the falls, resolute and rooted deep. The rising mist reaches me in waves, a rhythm as certain and precise as the soft open and close of butterfly wings. Nothing happens by chance, a friend told me once. Everything matters, she would say. It's a hypothesis that could take a lifetime to prove or disprove, and even then there's no guarantee of an answer. Even so, it may well be worth the effort.

The hike to Fern Lake covers about four miles in all, with a modest elevation gain of thirteen hundred feet. Along the way, I pass through various floral zones of ferns and shrubs and grasses. Because of the rugged terrain, the landscape here creates its own microclimate. During the summer, convectional storms occur almost on a daily basis. The result is more precipitation than what occurs down on the plains, a wetter climate altogether.

After a steep climb, the trail flattens out at the edge of the basin. From the rim of Fern Lake, I view the rampart of peaks to the west: Gabletop, Little Matterhorn, Knobtop, Notchtop. At the head of the valley, Grace Falls tumbles eighty feet in a dramatic veil of mist and snowmelt, draining the saddle of its runoff. Across the calm surface of the lake, shock waves expand in diminishing clarity.

Greenbacks.

I make camp near the lake, where the evergreens grow thick and close. I get it all ready for a return after dark, then gather rod and reel and walk down to a high bank overlooking the near shore. In the time it takes to assemble the rod, two cutthroat pass by the bank, pausing long enough to sip insects at the surface. A slight twist at the ferrule, the reel set firmly on the seat, I thread leader through the guides and listen for the clicking of flyline as it spins out from the reel.

I'll start with a fly given to me by a friend. I do this for luck, I suppose. If not for luck, then for something else that I may discover later on. If I'm lucky. He's done a good job with this attractor—tight wrap around the shank, bushy hackle. Blowing floatant through the white wings, I recall winter mornings spent in his university office surrounded by duck feather, elk hide, books, tying vise; frost forming on the inside of the window panes while patterns were tied, phone calls made for information on tailwater flows, trips schemed and pondered. All told, a welcome reprieve from the general affairs of everyday life. Like walking into a fly shop years ago, before the sport became fashionable and the pastime was not yet an industry—a dubious development that has led to a number of consequences, not the least of which was to push a few of the more cantankerous fishers to the remote backcountry in search of the solitude and meditation that drew them to the sport in the first place. Once upon a time, no matter where you found yourself, you could walk into a modest fly shop and feel as though you'd left the world behind. Walk off of any city street out of the noise and traffic, and know instantly that you'd found refuge. A safe haven of *troutness*.

On the second cast a healthy twelve-inch cutthroat takes the Orange Asher, running twice along the shore, twisting and veering for the deeper water. The trout turns and spins against the tension applied on the other end— tension that's not too heavy nor sustained for very long, because it's not the fight I'm after. Gradually, I work the cutthroat close enough to the bank to reach down and hold it in my hand. Removed from the camouflage of its natural habitat, the fish displays shocking colors. The dramatic red slash under the throat, a crimson streak running along the belly. Black oval spots across the tail, a tinge of gold and green along the lateral flanks. Remember this, I find myself thinking. All of it. Remember it like your life depends on it.

Every fisherman has his own story. A journey as personal and unique as a genetic code. This particular history, far from extraordinary, begins under a chrome Ohio sky with thoughts of bluegill, sunfish, and the occasional carp caught on a hook, string, and bamboo pole. A casting rod for Christmas and the range extends to the deeper holes, where catfish lurk in eutrophic roils of water so dirty it never occurred to anyone to actually swim there. Later, the neighborhood pond becomes Lake Michigan, downriggers replace bobbers, salmon supplant panfish. At about this time, too, a neighbor has a secondhand fly rod for sale. Cheap. He'll even throw in a box of flies. And then a late-summer morning on the Au Sable—in one of those pivotal moments of a boy's life when he catches a glimpse of his destiny—a ten-inch trout gets fooled by one of those flies, as both fish and river become forever etched in memory. Years later, the journey would move west to the Rocky Mountains for rainbow, cutthroat, and browns. Tailwaters mostly, catch and release. Until now, for reasons not always clear, alone to the high country and alpine lakes.

This migration from the Midwest to the Rocky Mountain backcountry might appear to indicate some pattern, some evidence of actual progress, but in truth any coherence to the years comes as a bit of a surprise. I have never thought of myself as a serious angler, never considered myself as all that accomplished. At each step of the way, I've watched others whose commitment and skill far surpassed my own. Great Lakes charter captains, for instance, who go out forty consecutive days. Rocky Mountain fly casters who don't miss a week of the year. That kind of dedication. Fishing, at least for those who still approach it as an avocation, begins to get interesting when the hobby turns to obsession. But if fishing never really reached this point for me, the years of dogged persistence have surely left their mark. Which leads me to believe that there's more to this than meets the eye. Even if we're convinced we can never grasp the full meaning of our lives, this doesn't preclude us from demanding an explanation. We seek causality, design. If the fishing itself yields few clues, we think, then maybe the *reasons* for fishing offer more insight. Indeed, these reasons can be every bit as compelling as the fishing itself. This is especially true in cases where the one compulsion may be superseded by another.

And just as the forms of fishing change over time, so too do the reasons. In the early years, as far as I could tell, soaking worms seemed like a good way to wile away the dog days of summer. Later, on Lake Michigan, trolling for coho and kings presented the perfect excuse to avoid all the nettlesome complications that awaited back on land. Later still, angling served a social function, a way to bridge some gap between people who should be close but aren't. Now, most of the time, I fish alone. And while it's difficult to pinpoint any reason for this, I believe it has to do with making a connection. A connection to the world, which for me begins with a connection to some natural place. If you're like me, you do this to give meaning to your life even if you don't entirely understand what it's about, but you do it anyway because something deep in your bones and blood tells you to. Or you do this because you want to *feel* something, anything at all, because maybe this is the point you've reached in life. And because you don't know any better, you look initially to make that connection in some tangible way like hooking native trout, knowing as you do that if this allows for some other kind of connection that you could not foresee, well, you'll be ready for it. Whatever it might be. A connection to the wild, to life, to the world. To yourself. On some level, you have to believe they all converge.

For the past two decades, I have called the Front Range of Colorado my home. A loose definition to be sure, but believing that home corresponds to a landscape of feeling more than anything else, I include in this designation the area extending roughly from the Fall River watershed in the north to Clear Creek canyon in the south. At least this much. East to west, the terrain is defined by a dramatic rise in elevation from the Great Plains to the Continental Divide—from about five thousand feet to fourteen thousand feet—with a lot of geographic folds and undulations in between. It can be a rough place, especially at the higher elevations: cold, windy, rugged. *Hostile*, to use the old vernacular. It's an area that also coincides with the native habitat of *Oncorhynchus clarki stomias*, the greenback cutthroat trout.

The greenback is one of at least fourteen subspecies of cutthroat trout native to the American West. In terms of native range, the cutthroat is by far the most widely distributed trout in the West, extending from central New Mexico north to southern Alberta and from the Pacific Ocean east to the Front Range. The greenback is native to the mountain and foothill streams of the Arkansas and South Platte river drainages, an area that falls almost entirely within the state of Colorado. Today, the greenback cutthroat survives in the only places it can. Pushed to the remote backcountry, the species inhabits a few alpine lakes and feeder creeks in what amounts to a fraction of its original range. Like other cutthroat species, the greenback requires a certain minimum standard of environmental quality. The presence of cutthroat indicates a sufficient supply of calcium, potassium, nitrate, phosphate, and carbon dioxide. It signifies a healthy and abundant insect population, and a temperature regime defined by daily and annual extremes. It means that the water oxygenation is at least four to five parts per million, that a minimum flow exists in the creeks, and that adverse impacts from mining, grazing, and logging are negligible. These days, wherever you find greenbacks you're also likely to find eagles, osprey, ouzels, herons, and hawks. You can be fairly certain that somewhere close by are elk, bear, lions, beaver, martens, and bobcat. In many instances you'll be surrounded by old growth forests, krumholz, and Precambrian rock. Chances are, too, you'll be afforded plenty of solitude.

In the morning, twenty trout line up in the shallow riffles above the outlet to Fern Creek. Some occupy lanes in the faster current, while others stay high along the edge of the pool. I float a parade of nymphs past them all, but the trout don't react. Finally, I switch to a Royal Coachman and get a few greenback to rise in the pool. The Royal Coachman is a classic high-altitude attractor and one of my favorite patterns. Red and green along the body, handsome white wings and brown hackle, this fly complements the bold and radiant colors of native cutthroat.

Greenbacks are not so gullible that they don't require a steady variety of flies. In this regard they are like other trout. On the other hand, given the harsh conditions of their habitat and the short feeding season, these cutthroat can't afford to be as selective as their cousins in more temperate climes. Throughout the day, various hatches follow each other like clockwork: baetis, caddis, big mayfly. The surface activity ebbs and flows on the lake, peaking when the sun slips behind the clouds and the wind subsides. After a number of refusals with an Orange Asher, I tie on a #14 Redquill Mayfly that immediately elicits a strike. The cutthroat veers for the protection of a rock shelf as I angle the rod to keep the fish clear. It's a healthy eleven-inch greenback, more silver than green, not as much red. Female, if I had to guess. Good fighter. Swallowed the fly whole, too, enough to require the hemostats to free the hook. I'll catch a half dozen more on this single fly, sight casting from a large boulder at the edge of the lake, watching for nearby rises or cruising trout along the bank.

As much as selecting the right fly pattern and size, presentation is crucial to this kind of fishing: a soft landing, momentary drift, the occasional strip to excite any nearby fish. It's always useful to present the fly in a place where the surface reflects the far bank rather than the bright sky. Against a dark background, a fisher can see a cutthroat rise to the fly or roll away at the last instant. Sometimes, a slight movement in the reflection might be mistaken for a rising trout, as the fly caster must then pause to regain his composure in the few seconds it takes for his heart to restore its rhythm. It's a quick and sudden thrill, this psychic jolt, which never seems to lose its charge no matter how many times it happens. On the other hand, stare long enough at the quicksilver skylight wending across the lake surface, and you're bound to feel yourself on the verge of some enchantment. If fly fishing can be described as an attempt to enter the world of trout, then maybe it's here that the exchange is possible, in this ephemeral medium of light and water.

A steady rain falls in the afternoon. I elect to wait it out in the cover of spruce and fir until the weather clears, and I return again to the boulder.

Adorned in silver and auburn lichen, the wet rock glistens as splintered sunlight angles deep into the emerald water below. Standing on top of the rock, the sun to my back, a shadow falls across this corona of light in the lake. It's my own silhouette I see, catching me by surprise.

HEART LAKE (11,300'), LATE JUNE

Initially, this idea to fish for greenback cutthroat grew out of a desire to explore some of the backcountry along the Front Range. As time went on and I got to see more of the area, I began to consider the notion of what it means to be rooted in a particular place, a place one might even call home. But before I could do this with any sincerity, I knew I had to come to terms with my own transient past. Mine is a history of regular relocation, a fact I once thought unfortunate and maybe even unnatural. And as I thought about my own experience, I began to consider the wandering habits of people in general. After all, migration has always been part of the human experience. Which got me thinking about the past and our ancestors, all those hominid forebears who for hundreds of thousands of years roamed the earth. In fact, anthropologists now believe that the evolutionary innovation that separated hominids from apes was none other than bipedality—the ability to walk on two legs in an upright posture.

If you subscribe to the land bridge theory, then you accept the hypothesis that Homo sapiens first migrated to North America some seventeen thousand years ago across an exposed land bridge connecting Siberia to Alaska. This would have occurred during the last ice age when sea levels were hundreds of feet lower than what they are today. Recent discoveries in both North and South Americas suggest that humans may have arrived on the continent even before then. However and whenever our ancestors arrived, the point is that we come from a long line of travelers. All of which raises the interesting possibility that perhaps we are not meant to stay in one place. Maybe we are all just footloose wanderers at heart, engineered to be on the move like all other migratory beasts of the world. Why, even plants will seek out greener pastures if given the chance. Maybe all this clamor about putting down roots is just wishful thinking. A pipe dream. Just the latest instance of one mythology taking the place of another.

Today, with Heart Lake as my destination, I too am on the move. Though my journey pales in comparison to that of our forebears, it is not without its own epic qualities. Starting at 5,200 feet altitude and climbing to 11,340 feet, I'll begin the day immersed in radio waves and digital technology and gradually work my way back to turn-of-the-century railroads, frontier cabins, old growth forest, and Precambrian granite. Along the way, I'll move from grassland plains to montane and subalpine forest and eventually onto alpine tundra. And, who knows, maybe the journey assumes a personal significance as well—a movement toward some primal self perhaps, deeper into some netherland of archaic consciousness.

The hike begins at the East Portal of the Moffat Tunnel. Completed in 1927, the tunnel runs six miles under the Continental Divide, connecting the rail line between Rollinsville and Winter Park. I find the trailhead along South Boulder Creek in the shadow of the valley. The trail winds through willow stands, past aspen groves and towering spruce trees at the edge of meadows. Rusted cable and flattened metal litter the ground, vestiges of old prospecting ventures. A few shacks persevere in the protective windbreaks of thick evergreens, cowering it seems before the anticipated ravages of wind and winter. One such tin-and-tarpaper shack sports an upside-down muffler for a stovepipe. The trail crosses the creek, bisecting a meadow where an abandoned homestead has been reclaimed now by cow parsnip, skunkbrush, chokecherry, harebells, and lupine. At the lower end of the meadow, the timbers of a tumbledown cabin lay jackstrawed in the grass. A side trail leads to a historic burial plot marked by what appear to be shallow graves. But I don't stay long. Somewhere at the head of the valley near the Divide, cutthroat are cruising the sunny flats of Heart Lake.

The path begins a long, steady climb into the heart of a mixed forest where the ground pitches around big granite boulders. I step across broad flats of white and pink quartz, but it's the trees I find most impressive. Trees of all sizes and stages. Blowdown and deadfall and snags at all phases of decomposition. One fallen trunk, stripped of its bark, stands nearly to my waist. Squiggly beetle tracks run helter-skelter across its smooth face like some cryptic hieroglyphic. They say it takes as long for a log to completely decompose as it does to live its entire life. If that's so, this log should still be here centuries from now. From a lower zone of aspen, ponderosa, and spruce, I pass into a montane forest of Douglas fir, limber pine, and Engelmann spruce. Witch's broom, a silver mossy epiphyte, drapes most of the trees. Shafts of luminous sunlight pour through the canopy, especially near the creek. A solitary junco glides through the forest to a fir branch down the hill.

Like the creek that it follows, the trail splits and braids in different directions. It's easy to get turned around in here. Did I veer onto a tributary just now and not know it? I keep to the main trail, crossing a sumpy meadow where the footpath forks near an old Forest Service sign that has long since been destroyed. Just as well. Too many signs as it is. How easily we allow ourselves to get tangled up in names and numbers. Labels. Better to break free of the restrictive matrix, to get beyond the safety of symbols and all the many prerogatives they impose, even if it means getting lost. Which is what I managed to do here last fall, following the drainage to Clayton Lake instead. Wandering around in two feet of snow, toes growing numb, I eventually reached Heart Lake only to find it already frozen.

Just before the trail starts a steep ascent, I come across two collapsed cabins in the forest. The bigger of the two stands four feet high along one corner, where its notched logs fit nicely together. I notice a couple of rusty sixteen-penny spikes toenailed in a lower section, so with one hand I lift up on the top log just to test the construction. The log falls off its perch, rolling to a stop in the duff and loam.

Uh oh, now I've done it. Interfered with the natural order of things, left my mark on the history of the area. Now what? Should I restore the log to its rightful place on the wall? Will this minimize my intrusion? Mitigate my transgression?

Hang it. I leave the cabin and the opportunistic saplings growing between its walls, taking advantage of the space and sunlight. Let this be my omen: these tiny trees sprung from history's ruins. This reclamation of forest.

Up I go through juniper and kinnikinnick, crossing meadows rimmed with evergreens. I wrap my arms around the trunk of a fir—seven feet around, I estimate, 120 feet high. Snags stand rooted and upright in death, gnarled and rugose. Farther up, a pine grosbeak waits like a sentry at the edge of tree line. All the while, the south ridge of the valley gleams in golden sunlight a thousand feet above. The trail traverses a sedge meadow then cuts through an island of fir, rising finally to the basin of Heart Lake, where drops of lazy sunlight flare across the surface. The lake is green at its center, tannic brown around the shallow flats. Above the basin, the landscape rises in a series of ridges to the high snowpack of Rogers Pass. I rig the flyline near a dense stand of krumholz, tying a new leader with a bloodknot that actually holds on the first try. I assemble the rod, thread leader through the guides, and reach for a caddis in the box.

Long before our ancestors were here, early forms of western cutthroat began a migration of their own into the interior of North America. Inhabiting the northern Pacific Coast—from the Gulf of Alaska south to Humboldt Bay in northern California—these prehistoric fish penetrated inland waterways perhaps as early as eight million years ago. The ancient Columbia River, created as a drainage for volcanic lakes, provided one route of access for migrating trout and salmon. Before it was diverted to the Columbia drainage, the Snake River may have presented another open waterway in central California.

The historical distribution of cutthroat populations was largely determined by the configuration of waterways created by glacial activity. During the periods of warming between glacial advances, fish were able to penetrate the continent as stream flows and lake levels ran high. Retreating ice sheets created vast lakes that would sometimes overflow into adjacent drainages. Waterways that had once been isolated became interconnected. Rivers and streams were captured into new drainages. Headwater creeks migrated back and forth across low alluvial divides. During the periods of glaciation, ice and volcanic activity created barriers in the waterways that isolated populations long enough for different subspecies to evolve. Rivers were diverted or dammed, or they split their flows into separate drainages.

Although it's not clear when cutthroat arrived to the Front Range, or even how they got here, Robert J. Behnke has described possible routes of migration whereby early forms of cutthroat could have migrated eastward and eventually crossed the Continental Divide. In his work *Trout and Salmon of North America*, Behnke writes that ancestral cutthroats could have found their way from the Snake River drainage to the upper Green River system in at least two places. Before it was diverted into the Bonneville Basin some thirty thousand years ago, the Bear River was a tributary to the Snake River. The upper tributaries of the Bear are located in close proximity to tributaries of the Green in the Uinta Mountain Range. Ancestral cutthroat could have crossed into the Green drainage here. A second possible transfer site exists near the Greys and Hoback rivers, two tributaries of the Snake that both come very close to headwaters of the Green north of the Uintas.

Once established in the Green, cutthroat could have reached headwater tributaries along the Continental Divide at a number of places, including the headwaters of the Little Snake River in Wyoming, where it might have crossed into the South Platte drainage. Ancestral cutthroat might have also migrated up the Colorado River into the Eagle River whose headwaters approach the Divide at both Fremont Pass and Tennessee Pass, leading into the Arkansas River drainage. Forty miles downstream on the Arkansas, Trout Creek Pass opens to the east, providing a passage to South Park and the South Platte drainage.

Interestingly, the migration of people into the interior West may have followed some of the same routes used by migrating cutthroat. Anthropologists theorize that as glaciers receded at the end of the last ice age, Paleolithic humans traveled southward along a corridor that had formed between ice sheets at the eastern foot of the Canadian Rockies. The migration continued westward, they believe, along the Missouri River valley. This would have brought them to mountain passes leading into the Snake River plain and eventually to the Great Basin, which at the time was inhabited by camels, woolly mammoths, and saber-toothed tigers.

I wait on a rock near the outlet of Heart Lake. To the west, jagged peaks rise in a lapis sky. I listen as a rock tumbles from someplace high on the scarp, never once seeing it. A raven glides across the rugged amphitheater, its throaty chortle reverberant. Magnificent.

There's something primeval about all of this—surrounded by cutthroat and krumholz and granite, hard along timberline in the shadow of the Great Divide. I was wrong about the lake. It has more color than I first noticed. Copper along the edges, the lake fades from emerald to blue to indigo and black at its deepest center. I'm reminded of time and how unfathomable it seems the further we gaze from the familiar shores of the here and now.

The torpedoed shadows of two trout emerge from the deep, cruising along the bottom in four feet of water. I may get only one good chance at them, so the presentation has to be good—a soft delivery somewhere forward of their present course. I make two false casts and let it go, hearing the line run through the guides. The fly alights on the lake, starting a dimple across the surface. The first cutt doesn't move, but the far trout pivots and rises quickly to the fly, darting for the protective cover of rocks as its weight registers in my hand. The cutthroat makes three runs before I can get it close to the boulder. It measures only twelve inches, but it's a fine fish. Bright shades of red, green, gold, and black. I weave the trout gently in the water before it swims off slowly, fading back into the luminescent green.

Upper Hutcheson Lake (10,900'), Early July

Of the several subspecies of western cutthroat, the greenback has been described as the most colorful and beautiful of all—a fact I attribute to the harsh conditions of its native habitat, although this is only a personal theory. Aside from the signature red slash and gill flap, greenbacks tend to display considerable variation in color. Some appear silver coming out of the water, while others are distinctly green or even bronze. Some have a golden hue under the belly and along the ventral fins. Spawning males develop red coloration along the ventral region, in addition to the throat and gill flap.

Greenbacks typically possess the largest and most pronounced spots of any cutthroat, round to oblong in shape and concentrated on or near the tail. They also possess the highest scale count of any other cutthroat. Greenbacks are not big fish, seldom exceeding one to two pounds in weight and fifteen inches in length. They also appear to be strict invertebrate feeders, refusing fish flesh and commercial diets. Finally, greenbacks are perhaps the most vulnerable of all cutthroats, easily replaced by nonnative trout. Rare, beautiful, and vulnerable, greenbacks fit the profile of many other endangered species around the globe.

According to Behnke, the evolution of cutthroat can be traced as far back as a hundred million years when a split occurred in the oceanic fishes of the order Salmoniformes, resulting in a new family of Salmonidae. This family would eventually branch into three subfamilies during the Eocene: Coregoninae (whitefishes), Thymillinae (graylings), and Salmoninae (trouts, salmon, and chars). From this latter group, the genus *Oncorhynchus* would emerge. Eventually, two distinct lines developed in this genus: one that produced the Pacific salmons, and another that produced the western trouts, including rainbow and cutthroat. Though estimates vary, the split between rainbow and cutthroat may have occurred as early as eight million years ago.

It appears the first significant divergence in the cutthroat line occurred between a coastal cutthroat with sixty-eight chromosomes and a Columbia River cutthroat with sixty-six chromosomes. From this latter group, a third form evolved with only sixty-four chromosomes. This third form—inhabiting most of the Snake River section of the Columbia River drainage—would itself separate into two groups: one isolated in the Lahontan Basin that evolved into the Lahontan cutthroat, and a second that remained in the Snake River system and evolved into the largespotted Yellowstone cutthroat. Over time, six "minor" subspecies would emerge from the Yellowstone line, including the Colorado River cutthroat and the greenback cutthroat.

Today, taxonomists recognize fourteen subspecies of cutthroat trout based on genetic difference, each associated with a specific native habitat. Six of these subspecies are native to the Great Basin, three to the Rocky Mountain region of Colorado and New Mexico, and six others to Wyoming. Two subspecies, the yellowfin cutthroat and the Alvord cutthroat, have become extinct.

Behnke proposes that when receding waters put an end to headwater transfers along the Continental Divide eight thousand years ago, a population of Colorado River cutthroat became isolated in the Arkansas and South Platte drainages. Over the millennia, this isolated population adapted to the particular conditions of its new environment and eventually became the greenback cutthroat. Recent genetic tests suggest the divergence between greenback cutthroat and Colorado River cutthroat may have occurred much earlier, sometime between seven hundred thousand and two million years ago. Morphologically, the two subspecies look very much the same. Greenbacks tend to have higher scale counts and slightly different spotting than Colorado River cutthroat, but these tendencies are anything but conclusive. Behnke points out that, in terms of spotting and scale counts, Colorado River cutthroat native to the Little Snake River drainage in Wyoming look more like greenback cutthroat than they do other Colorado River cutthroat, leading him to believe that this was once a transfer site.

Located deep inside the backcountry of Wild Basin, the Hutcheson Lakes were once thought to be among the few places where relict greenback populations could be found. In fact, the Colorado Division of Wildlife used Upper Hutcheson Lake as a broodstock source for greenbacks up until 1995. Although recent tests indicate the population may not be as pure as once believed, the Hutcheson Lakes maintain a sense of the high and wild. This is about as remote as one can get along the Front Range anymore. The nine-mile hike to Upper Hutcheson is measured not in terms of distance or time, but by natural features seen along the way: the ponderosa and aspen meadow filled with black-eyed Susans and bluebells, the sweep of high peaks off to the north and west, the verdant basin of Finch Lake, the ascent across snowfields to the base of Mount Copeland.

Situated at the southern edge of Rocky Mountain National Park, Wild Basin bears the evidence of millions of years of geomorphology. The uplift of the Rockies, which began between sixty-five and seventy million years ago, continued until at least seven million years ago and perhaps as recently as five million years ago. Wind, water, and ice have slowly shaped the mountains into their present appearance. The Paleozoic and Mesozoic sedimentary rocks, so prevalent in the foothills, have entirely eroded away at the higher elevations, exposing large batholithic masses of Precambrian granite and metamorphics. Infusions of Tertiary quartz appear in the rock in the form of sills, dikes, and stocks. But the most significant influence on the topography of Wild Basin has been the glacial activity that has carved much of the Rockies over the past two million years. Today, we see evidence of these glaciers in the U-shaped valleys, cirques, and morainal deposits.

Sometimes, while hiking the high tundra flats along the Divide, I'll look off in the distance to such faraway places as the Gore Range, the Never Summers, or Rabbit Ears, and think of things I did there. Invariably, I'll think of the friends with whom I shared the experience, as I'm transported through memory to another time and place. But it's there along the crest line, too high for glaciers ever to reach, where the feeling occurs, rarely below, where glaciers have gnashed and fractured the land. Call it a flatlander's sensibility, but down below, the rock is too severely broken, the upheaval too recent, the landscape too raw and imposing. If there is any solace in these places, it's to be found in the delicate things: the song of a sparrow at tree line, a spider web catching morning sunlight in its concentric strands, the white shock of marsh marigolds at the foot of a snowfield. Maybe I am drawn to these things because they remind me of my own precarious purchase on this earth, my own tenuous existence in the face of such daunting power. A power, I have to say, that fascinates as much as it repels.

Fishing on Pear Lake, my camp for the night, I'll wonder about such matters and what it is exactly that compels a fisher to his pursuit. What drives the fascination? At one point, inspired by the surroundings perhaps, I'll consider our own genetic circuitry and an evolutionary past that has its origins in the sea. As humans, we descended from marine organisms by way of a long journey that involved amphibians, reptiles, and other mammals. As fishers, then, are we really just engaged in a symbolic return to these watery origins? On the other hand, consider the millions of years our hominid ancestors plied their skills as hunters. Surely, somewhere deep within our psychic wiring, such predatory instincts persist. How much of this, then, is genetically determined? To what extent can we explain fishing as ritualistic behavior designed to channel primitive impulses? And while we're on the subject, how many of these coded responses have been rendered inappropriate by the conditions and demands of the modern world we now inhabit?

Night falls under an overcast sky, dark and windy. The light of the fire carries only twenty feet or so to the edge of the forest. Beyond that, a wall of darkness waits at the periphery, thick and brooding. Somewhere out there, not far away, the last of my food hangs from a tree limb. I've made camp on a small bench above Pear Lake, where I settle in late with a cigar and brandy—a kind of ritual I sometimes share with myself when camping alone. Pear Lake is the last camp on the south trail into Wild Basin. Tomorrow, I'll bushwhack the final two miles to Upper Hutcheson Lake.

The wind rustles the spruce boughs overhead, as I add another scrap of deadfall to the fire. The sough of wind through evergreen needles sounds both soothing and plaintive, like a whispered lament I can't fully understand. The Iroquois had a story for this. They spoke of a young woman's death song, heard among the roar of rapids as she approached her fateful end. The Iroquois had other stories, too. The wail of a loon conveyed the voice of a fallen warrior caught between worlds. Aurora borealis reflected the light of bonfires enjoyed by festive warriors in the hereafter. D. H. Lawrence wrote that the American landscape was haunted by Indian spirits and would remain so until such spirits were appeased by a transformation of consciousness that incorporated Native elements. How else to explain the restlessness, malaise, and madness of the white American soul? Not until we find our proper place among these spirits, Lawrence thought, can we ever expect to establish a lasting connection to the land.

The wind howls, the fire breathes. I take another drink. Like the wind, my imagination is on the loose tonight.

It occurs to me that today marks the anniversary of Hemingway's death. And now they've just found the body of his granddaughter badly decomposed, dead too by her own hand. The list of suicides in the family is impressive: Hemingway, his father, sister, brother, and now this latest at forty-one. If, as Camus said, there is but one truly serious philosophical problem and that is suicide, then maybe we should just leave it at that. Out here tonight in these woods, any moral redress on the subject seems to miss the point entirely. Maybe at the end, Hemingway could sense he was losing his nerve. The sessions of shock treatment probably didn't help matters, though depression is a hell of a thing. There was the drinking, too. On the other hand, making a career out of pushing the edge is bound to exact a toll. In the face of death is freedom, wrote John Killinger. "Nothing has any meaning at that instant except survival and existence. The superfluities of culture, race, tradition, even religion, all disappear in the face of one overpowering fact—the necessity to exist on an individual basis." There's just one catch to this credo: the near-death experience must be repeated again and again for life to continue to have meaning. The encounter with violence or death must be continually re-created, ritualized even.

Today, psychologists speak of the emotional and biochemical rewards associated with such encounters—the sense of euphoria that follows a confrontation with death and fear. They compare the mental concentration that occurs at these moments to a religious state of transcendence. Fueled by the release of natural endorphins, this concentration produces a state of calm and tranquillity, a clarity of purpose. Applying one's skill and knowledge in a situation of self-imposed stress increases the sense of control over one's destiny. An experience of acute risk taking, they say, strips away the dross of historical man. There is only time for reaction, an informed intuitive response. But like the existential moment of truth, the biochemical rewards of risk taking last only so long. The experience of risk must be duplicated again and again. And whether we describe these encounters in philosophical or psychological terms, the reality is that no amount of fancy rhetoric can take the place of the experience. It has to be lived in order to be understood.

But already the words grow tiresome. Glib.

Add another log to the fire, take another drink. Think of something else, something more to the point, like Ad Francis taking a blackjack to the back of the head in "The Battler." Now there's a thought. It's like Lawrence himself said: don't trust the artist, trust the work. What remains in the final analysis is the writing. Even now, the images ring true: Nick trailing his hand through the lake at sunrise in "Indian Camp." The whitecaps on Lake Michigan beyond the wooded point in "The Last Good Country." The mosquito and the flame in "Big Two Hearted River." Images that endure through the years, keeping company—clear as a summer sky after a strong north wind. Like the peace, I suppose, earned after putting your neck on the line one more time.

And so I raise my glass to the ghost of Ernest Hemingway. Here's to you, old bastard. Here's to wildness and ruin, to taking risks and all the hell that goes with it. Here's to demons and freedom, and to whichever comes first.

In the morning, I follow a footpath along the south side of Pear until I lose it under a field of snow. At that point I turn my attention to the dog-eared topo I've brought along and navigate according to its lines of elevation. Rising to a plateau, I pass a shallow pond and continue south through a forest of giant spruce to the fast rapids of Cony Creek. From here, I turn upstream and head west for the Divide. The hiking is tough at times, especially with all the deadfall, marshes, krumholz, and fellfields to negotiate.

State biologists once traveled this same route on their way to gathering spawn from the cutthroat of Upper Hutcheson. It's this notion of the pristine that has brought me here. Nine miles from the trailhead, eleven thousand feet above sea level, I should expect to find some sense of the wild in this high backcountry. Granted, it's always a dicey affair to expect nature to conform to some ideal of the mind. Tragedies occur for less. Yet, rising from the forest to the tundra and the broken country beyond, I have to believe I'm getting close to some vital essence, some unique distillate of what evolution has concocted here over the course of millions of years. Above Lower Hutcheson is Middle Hutcheson, and above that, Upper Hutcheson. Above Upper Hutcheson is Cony Lake, a glacial tarn, which sits at the base of Cony Glacier. Beyond that, there's only the crest of the Divide and mountains of clouds rising in the sky.

Cony Creek flows from basin to basin, following a staircase of lateral glacial deposits left behind from the great rivers of ice that once moved down this valley. I fish as I go, ever mindful of the principle that drives me onward that may or may not hold any meaning in the end. The landscape may be pristine, but it makes for difficult walking; the greenbacks may be wild and remote, but just pretty to look at in the final analysis. I see no surface activity on Lower Hutcheson, so I sight cast to passing trout. Even underwater, the fish exhibit startling coloration. Against an emerald backdrop, these cutthroat display a copper color that blends to scarlet along the ventral fins and belly. From the boulder field, I catch a healthy twelve-inch greenback with all the classic markings: red fins and gill flap, large oval spots near the tail and dorsal fin, a faint lateral streak of red, lesser silver spots on a background of bronze.

Above Lower Hutcheson, the trees begin to scatter as I cross a grassy flat overlooking the lake. My strategy is to stay high along the valley slope, above the gorges and marshes and dense shrub growing along the creek. From the tundra slope, I can see the bright snowfield of Cony Glacier below the pass and the creek as it winds through the valley, connecting a chain of boulder ponds like a string of jewels. Fields of scree and tundra descend eastward to tree line and the upper reaches of spruce and fir. I see it all—from the snowy pass to the dazzling lakes to the blue ridges of distant foothills and the Great Plains beyond. And the wildflowers: alpine poppy, columbine, Arctic gentian, elephanthead, American bostort, rose crown, Indian paintbrush, purple aster, chiming bells...too many to count. A gust of wind starts a wave across the shimmering meadow when suddenly the yellows and blues and ochers take flight on the wings of sulphur, fritillary, and blue butterflies. In pockets of shade, fly agaric blossoms fat and round like baked apples. Lion signs are everywhere, leaving little doubt whose home this really is. Wending my way through thick krumholz, I discover a single paw print sunk deep in the mud, wide enough to hide a baseball. And rock. Scarps, turrets, benches, fellfields, scree, slabs…rock of endless shape and size, of every color and swirly infusion. There's an intelligence to all this, a beautiful necessity. Everything is in its place as it should be, without so much as an afterthought to man—if you exclude what appears to be the strategic placement of lion scat in the middle of the path.

At Upper Hutcheson, I rig rod and reel with ten feet of leader and a #18 Adams. This lake looks clearer, more colorful than any I've seen in the Colorado backcountry. Aqua along the sandy shallows, the water blends to a deep green beyond the rocky shelf. A trout darts from the near bank. The lake is loaded with rising cutthroat, and I know it's just a matter of getting the fly close. Fishing from the rocks I cast to passing greenback, watching for the larger fish and the twenty-inch lunker rumored to be lurking in the frigid depths. The cutthroat of Upper Hutcheson are healthy, colorful, above average in size, and easily caught. Spawning males show red along the belly, fading to gold, then to olive at the dorsal and adipose fins. Many of the smaller fish have parr marks and, for some, a faint streak of red along the sides.

I inadvertently tangle fly and leader during a cast, requiring ten minutes or so of close attention. Looking up again, I see the cutthroat have resumed their feeding in the rocky shallows along the bank. A larger trout passes by, fanning its pectoral fins. From thirty feet away, I put the Adams just off its nose with half the leader falling on the rocks. Not a difficult cast by most standards, but still pleasing to the eye. The trout circles and rises to the fly. At fifteen inches, it may be the biggest greenback I'll ever catch.

For the better part of an hour, I've been making my way down the bank toward a large boulder at the inlet where scores of trout are feeding on a hatch of callibaetis. With their handsome gossamer wings riding high in the air, the baetis look like tiny windjammers scudding across the water. I sneak up to the rock and wait. Behind me, a cascade of snowmelt sings in the rarefied air. Shadows from high outcrops fall across the glacier beneath the jagged crest line of Elk Tooth and Ogallala. The snowfield is streaked with the tracks of fallen slabs below the cornice. Soon the snows will begin again, hardly three months from when they last fell. Upper Hutcheson will freeze as it has for eons. The greenback will hunker down, metabolism low, feeding off the bottom on nymphs.

But for now, white spinnakers of cloud sail over the scarp, close enough to almost touch. The wind quickens and sweeps down over the lake. A shadow descends, and the trout stop feeding. I wait with barbless hook pinched between finger and thumb. The cloud moves away. The wind settles. Upper Hutcheson becomes transparent again in aqua blue. Everything comes clear, as a dozen cutthroat rise to the new light.

ROARING RIVER (9,300'), EARLY AUGUST

Of all the many advantages to fly fishing, a few deserve special mention. Aside from its meditative benefits, fly fishing provides an intimate look into the natural world. It allows you to lose the crowds (if you let it), it doesn't cost much (again, if you let it), and it gets you into some of the more beautiful places around. Still another appealing aspect is the latitude and freedom it affords to *personalize* the experience. You can fish for what you like, where you like, and generally go about it in a way that suits your pleasure. Indeed, there are a number of approaches and forms to choose from. For instance, a fly caster can fish either above or below the surface, selecting from an array of larva, pupa, nymph, emergent, and adult patterns to imitate the various stages of insect life. If he has a mind to, he can fish year-round in virtually any weather or water condition: ice out, tailwaters, spring creeks, ponds, lakes, streams, flats, blue water. Moreover, he or she can invent, borrow, or improve upon any number of strategies or techniques: rollcast, backcast, stripping, wading, floating, bellyboating, crawling through the grass so the big-bastard-feeding-along-the-bank doesn't see you.

Located at the base of the Mummy Range, Roaring River offers classic small-creek fishing. This is quite a departure from still-fishing in lakes. In a lake, where the water is stationary and often calm, most fish are on the move—cruising the banks and shelves. Conversely, in a fast-flowing stream where the riffles are stationary, the fish tend to hold in the current, sometimes veering up or downstream to a pocket or eddy where they don't have to expend as much energy. A particularly fast and steep mountain creek, Roaring River drains a number of high-country lakes: Ypsilon, the Spectacles, Chiquita, Lawn. In 1982, a major flood roared down this drainage after a dam burst at Lawn Lake.

Sediment from the flood washed into the valley and created the "Alluvial Fan" along Fall River, which in turn created Fan Lake. The flood cut a broad swath through the canyon, evidenced by the wide sandbars and scoured banks. Thirty feet *above* the river, flood debris still clings to the cutbanks along the edge of the forest. Some of these woody tangles are as big as log cabins. Fifteen years after the deluge, seedlings and saplings find anchorage along the sandbar. Yellow sulphur, purple aster, and fireweed bloom on the alluvial flat.

I work my way upstream, holding the rod high, letting the wind carry both line and leader to a smooth pillow of water where I let the fly down gently. I call this "wind casting," which really requires only a subtle maneuver of the rod. I use a #14 hopper on a twelve-foot leader, since grasshoppers have been snapping through the air all day. There's nothing quite like hopper fishing for the average fly caster—big robust splashes, fast aggressive strikes. Like the purple aster, hopper fishing signals a particular time of year when summer has settled down and become comfortable with itself. Hot clear days, crisp starlit nights, low flows, rising trout. Indeed, a Colorado angler can measure the seasons according to a cycle of notable hatches: caddis on the Arkansas, stone flies on the Colorado, green drakes on the Frying Pan, trichos on the South Platte. A particular fly pattern calls to mind a specific time of year, a certain stretch of river.

Some holes and runs on Roaring River are big enough to provide two or three lanes for holding trout. But the greenback are wary here; they sense your presence quickly. You have one, maybe two chances to present the fly before the fish is onto you. If you haven't made a good presentation by then, you might as well pick up and move on. Which is one of the beauties of creek fishing. You simply walk a few paces upstream to get a fresh start of things, a new lease on life. And so I advance from pocket to pocket, wind casting when the breeze is right, sometimes casting downstream to avoid drag. It's imperative to keep the rod high, allowing only a few inches of leader to touch the creek. Otherwise the line catches in the faster current, pulling the fly across the river, raising a wake like a speedboat. Even a greenback, whose intelligence will never excite even the most ardent ichthyologist, knows enough to avoid such an aberration as this.

On one cast, a greenback slams the hopper just as it settles on the water. The trout runs a bit and I let it go, watching that it doesn't veer behind a log where the line might tangle or break. Eventually, I coax the cutthroat close and free the hook. The fish remains near my feet, close enough for me to reach down and touch it again. When it swims away I groom the hopper fly, hook it in the cork of the rod butt, and make my way upstream. I follow a path above the cutbank through aspen groves and shaggy fir, blowdown and exposed boulders. Kinnikinnick grows along the forest floor among the trees. Magpies and jays and nutcrackers trumpet my passing.

Returning to the creek I sit down in the sand to change flies, searching through the pockets of my old Orvis vest, retrieving an expired fishing license by mistake. From five years ago, no less. Someday I must clean out these pockets and discard all the old licenses, cigar wraps, scraps of monofilament; put loose split shot and strike indicators back in their proper places. Why hang on to all these expired licenses, anyway? Why haven't I thrown them out by now?

The sun shines, the fish aren't going anywhere. I could probably have some luck with a midge or brassie dropper, but it's August and I refuse to nymph. I've caught my share as it is and shouldn't expect the fishing to be that much different the rest of the afternoon. Sitting by the creek, glints of mica flashing in the sun, I gather all the old licenses from my vest and lay them in the sand—arranging the expired Colorado tags with the nonresident licenses I've collected. *Chama, Jensen, Jackson, Dillon.* I spread them out in front of me where I can see them all, and for a moment, the random years seem to fall into place. *Ennis, Salmon, Dubois, Kernville.* Maybe I've seen some of the West after all, enough anyway to get a sense of things. In this makeshift arc of crumpled fishing tags, this record of where I've been, I find a texture to the years. A solid ground beneath the flowing waters of time. In a stream deep enough to be a life half gone.

Diamond Lake (10,900'), Mid-August

Closer to home now, whatever that might be and all that it may include.

My own sense of what it means has changed over the years, dictated by shifting circumstances, things ventured and lost. For those of us who by default or design have had to reconfigure the concept, *home* has come to mean something beyond the traditional associations of house and family, friends and community. For many, it has come to include a relationship with the land, an affinity not only for its scenic qualities but for the entire constituency of plants and animals, rock and water, air and ground. And as we broaden the concept, we shouldn't lose sight of the traditional values associated with home: faith, trust, love, respect. The ties that bind.

Diamond Lake sits in a basin above the valley floor of the North Fork of Boulder Creek, one mile from the Divide as the raven flies. I've walked this path before on my way to Arapaho Glacier, passing remnants of the old Fourth of July Mine at the head of the valley. Both the glacier and pass are named for the people who lived here before Europeans arrived. Along with the Ute and Cheyenne, the Arapaho hunted in the high country and traveled the mountain passes on their way to and from the western slope. The Commanche and Kiowa also lived along the Front Range, primarily on the plains and in the foothills.

The first Europeans to see the Front Range were probably Spanish explorers, traveling north from Santa Fe in the early eighteenth century in search of gold and silver. French traders also may have reached the Front Range by the eighteenth century. James Purcell, one of the first white Americans to explore the Rockies, journeyed in 1803 up the South Platte River, where he was eventually captured by Kiowas in South Park. Three years later, he would tell Zebulon Pike of the gold he found at the headwaters of the Platte.

By the early 1800s, French and American fur trappers had explored many of the main river drainages along the Front Range. For all intents and purposes, they were the only white men to visit the area, often traveling alone and living with Indians during the winter months. The lucrative fur industry attracted speculators from back east who established trading posts on the rivers along the plains. But when fashions changed and silk replaced fur as the preferred material in men's hats, the price of beaver plummeted. By the late 1840s, all the trading posts were abandoned. Then in 1858, William Green Russell led a mining expedition to Cherry Creek near the present site of Denver. His discovery of gold there would change the history of the Front Range forever.

The Diamond Lake trail begins near an abandoned road at the bottom of the valley, close to a government sign proclaiming "no public use." I elect to use it anyway, proceeding along the old two-track that, according to my topo, intersects the main trail only a mile or so up the valley. Halfway there, the road narrows to a footpath and then disappears altogether, forcing me to bushwhack along the south valley wall, using the Diamond Creek waterfall as a landmark. This stubborn insistence to take the way less traveled has gotten me into trouble more than once. Experience teaches it pays to stay on the trail. On the other hand, getting off the beaten path has led me to some pretty interesting places.

The mesic forest displays a dense understory of ferns, bitterbrush, and skunkbrush. Sunlight slants between spruce and fir in the misty, luminescent air. Leaves of cow parsnip have turned gold in the clearings below, a harbinger of autumn. I follow animal trails across the valley slope, marked by deer prints and bear tracks. Elk, black bear, mountain lion, mule deer, bobcat, coyote, red and gray fox, marten, and weasel call this place home. Recently, moose have moved in. And there are others: squirrel, chipmunk, marmot, pika, ptarmigan, magpie, Steller's jay, Clark's nutcracker, goldfinch, grosbeak, ouzel, raven, eagle, hawk, vulture. And their cousins, gone now but not forgotten: grizzly bear, timber wolf, bison, antelope, wolverine, otter, badger, mountain goat, lynx. All are native to the area. Some in body, others in spirit. All are strands in the great fabric of homeplace.

I pick up the main trail where it winds through meadows of purple aster and paintbrush, and follow it out to Diamond Lake. The far ridge of the valley gleams in autumn colors: burnt orange, gold, copper. The lake is shallow along the north end, so I work my way past the outlet to the south bank. The wind blows cold over Mount Neva, as a low pushes in from the northwest. Wind is a given here, along with weather of all kinds. Sometimes, when the sun shines and the wind subsides, this alpine country can seem positively serene. Most of the time, though, it strikes me as fundamentally *inhuman*— a place where I remain very much the visitor. Which is part of the appeal. It's no accident a person can find solitude up here. If it's wind and rock and cold to which I must ally myself, so be it.

Keeping low, I cast along the bank to the deeper water just off the shelf, letting a Royal Wulff drift in the wavelets. A tiny swirl disturbs the surface, followed by a flash of white in the deep. The fish makes two good runs before

I get him close. It's a thirteen-inch cutthroat: black spots along the tail, red along the belly and gill flap, with a slight golden hue coming out of the water. The hooked lower jaw gives it a primeval countenance.

Maybe it's the wind or the change in air pressure, but the trout are off the surface today. Out of more of the same stubbornness, no doubt, I refuse to fish muddlers—working my way along the bank instead with the same attractor, earning nothing for my efforts but a few refusals. Eventually, I hook another cutthroat, a female from the looks of it: dim red lateral streak, silver coloring, two red slashes under the head. I can feel my fingers go numb when I release the fish back into the lake. Marmots and pikas bark from the boulder field along the water. You have to admire these rodents, sticking it out in these harsh conditions. It takes a special resilience, a certain obstinacy on their own part.

One more fish now, before I pack it in and head out.

After Russell and his party discovered gold at Cherry Creek, they sent samples of their find back to Kansas City before heading north to continue their quest. By the time they returned to the plains a few months later, they found new cabins built near the site of their original strike. Soon, more gold was discovered at Gold Run and along Clear Creek near the present towns of Black Hawk and Central City. That same year, Denver was founded and became the first permanent white settlement along the Front Range. By late 1859, gold was being mined in many of the streams along the Front Range from the Cache la Poudre south to the Arkansas. A dozen boomtowns sprang up along the foothills, with names like Boulder and Golden. At least twenty-eight mining, logging, and supply camps started up in Boulder County alone. Within two years after Russell's find, more than one hundred thousand prospecting "fifty-niners" had descended on the Front Range, many of whom remained after the mining went bust.

It didn't take long for native cutthroat to feel the effects of this economic boom. With the exception of yellowfin cutthroat in Twin Lakes, the greenback was the only trout species to inhabit the Arkansas and South Platte drainages when the first whites ventured west to Colorado. Early reports suggest that it flourished in great numbers throughout its native range. But with the discovery of gold, the area along the eastern foothills became a major center of population and agriculture. Stream flows were diverted and depleted to meet the needs of farms and towns. The adverse effects of mining pollution, logging, and livestock grazing deteriorated the habitat and decimated local cutthroat populations. To this day, no cutthroat have been seen in Clear Creek since the discovery of gold there in 1859. Trout were also harvested to feed the thousands of miners living in isolated mountain camps. Market fishing became something of its own industry during the gold rush, leading to the dubious practice of dynamiting streams.

By the 1880s, cutthroat populations throughout the West had declined so dramatically that many states and territories enacted laws to protect native trout, though enforcement of these laws was virtually nonexistent. Ironically, efforts to improve western fisheries in the late nineteenth century may have had the most devastating effect of all. Concerned over the dwindling numbers of cutthroat, local officials and sporting clubs launched a campaign to restore the quality of fishing. Game and fish commissions were established, and hatcheries were constructed to supply western waters with stocked trout. As a result, exotic species—including nonnative cutthroat—were introduced to western streams and lakes.

Rainbow trout ultimately became the species of choice in western hatcheries. Planted by the millions, the more aggressive rainbows hybridized with native cutthroat, eliminating what remained of many wild populations. Brook trout and German browns were also introduced. Though these trout don't interbreed with cutthroat, they easily outcompete native cutts in a common habitat. All of these exotic species were transported to the West primarily by the railroads. In fact, railroad companies often provided free travel to state and federal hatchery personnel in exchange for stocking trout in local waterways along the rail lines. The railroads and towns they supplied would then advertise sportfishing to attract anglers from across the nation. By the turn of the century, remnant cutthroat populations throughout the West survived only in the most remote headwater creeks of the high mountains. The situation became so dire for native cutthroats along the Front Range that, by 1937, the greenback was thought to be extinct.

I cast with the wind, down to a small cove at the corner of the lake. The fly drifts across the edge of the shelf when a trout hits it hard, a strike unlike the others. I play it safe, careful not to break the fish off, giving it line when it wants to run. It darts twice for the deeper water, before I work it across the shelf to the bank where I see the markings for the first time: blue and white spots, fiery orange fins.

It's a brookie. A low-down, exotic *eastern brook trout*.

Geez, now what? I know biologists insist that anglers harvest brook trout in certain greenback waters in order to give native cutts a fighting chance. But what about here at Diamond, just another out-of-the-way backcountry lake? It's not his fault he's a brookie. His instinct tells him to live, and lord knows that's hard enough to do up here. All that ethical exercising about genetic purity hardly seems to matter just now. And look how pretty, what with all the vermilion and turquoise, the black and white stripes.

The fish slithers in my hand. Clouds amass over the Divide. The wind picks up a notch. I need to make a decision. From the boulder field behind me, the marmots continue their incessant chatter.

Ah, the marmots.

Yellow-bellied marmot (*Marmota flaviventris*): denizen of high-country fellfields; believed to subsist on roots, herbs, grasses, and the occasional piscatory scavenge.

In the interest of science, I break the neck of *Salvelinus fontinalis* and respectfully offer it to *M. flaviventris*.

LOCH VALE (10,200′), EARLY SEPTEMBER

The day begins auspiciously on my way through the tiny hamlet of Lyons. Driving through town, I see the proprietor of South Fork Ltd. (appointments only) standing outside the purple doorway of his renowned fly shop. For a few thousand bucks he'll handcraft a custom bamboo rod for you, made out of rare Tonkin cane shipped all the way from southeastern China. But you'll have to be patient. He only makes forty a year, and the wait time is about twice that. I wave to him as I drive through town, and he returns the greeting. I take it as an omen, a gesture of goodwill and camaraderie, though he has no idea who I am and I know of him only through literature. In fact, the Front Range enjoys a fairly rich fly fishing culture, if you consider the extended family of trout luminaries, past and present, who have called this place home. The names and personalities of local scribes, guides, and fly tiers are all familiar to me by now. If only vicariously through books, I feel somewhat connected to this loose community of trout bums, some of whom have parlayed their passion into full-time work, though this should not be held against them.

The destination today is Loch Vale, or "The Loch" as some call it, a popular day trip for tourists in Rocky Mountain Park. In fact, day hikers are already on the trail by nine in the morning, congregating near the trailhead and along scenic Alberta Falls. Below the falls, aspen trees grow in the cracks of large granite slabs. The trail winds through purple asters the size of silver dollars, Indian paintbrush, white and yellow daisies. At Chaos Canyon Cascades, ravens glide along the high cliff amid an amplified chorus of dissonant birdsong.

The view from Loch Vale is said to remind some of the Alps, though I've never been there myself. To the west, a rampart of snowy peaks rises in a vault of blue sky: Taylor Peak, Sharkstooth, Otis Peak. Taylor Glacier sits just below the crest line of the Divide, shining in morning sunlight. The Loch collects runoff from Andrews Tarn in the north, and from Sky Pond and Glass Lake in the south. All is beautiful on this heavenly day, though I hardly notice, transfixed as I am on what the trout are doing. Hands shaking with anticipation, I assemble the rod and ready a new leader. I'll start with a #18 Orange Asher. As with other alpine lakes, the strategy here entails a bit of stalking. It's all perfectly suited for the fishing purist: sight casting dry flies to native cutthroat in a wild and natural setting. On my third cast, I watch a fish rise to take the fly. I work the trout close and take note of the red slashes below the jaws, the cutthroat spotting and red gill flap, the faint lateral arc. It's always good to get the first fish out of the way, to put the collar away for the day.

Living in these harsh conditions, the trout aren't overly fussy. So long as the presentation is good, they don't seem to be as persnickety when it comes to a specific pattern of fly. Of course, like everything else in fishing, this is only sometimes true. Without notice, the surface activity suddenly stops, as I go a half hour without so much as a refusal. When the feeding resumes, I catch a number of cruising cutthroat on Asher, Adams, Henryville Caddis…anything small and dark, it seems. Why, at the end of the day, I'll even dip into the terrestrials and tie on a Blank Ant. I'll catch a nice twelve-inch trout on it, too, a fish that had been consistently rejecting my fat #16 Humpy.

I've been told there are cuttbows in The Loch, though recent genetic tests reveal no presence of rainbow. "Cuttbow" is a generic term used to describe a rainbow and cutthroat hybrid. Hybridization in native trout often results from the introduction of a closely related nonnative species. In the case of the greenback, hybridization occurred when spring-spawning rainbow and non-native cutthroats were introduced to Front Range streams and lakes beginning in the late nineteenth century. Although there may be no rainbow in the greenbacks of Loch Vale, geneticists have recently detected a trace presence of Yellowstone cutthroat.

Hybridization between trout species can occur in varying degrees, depending on the extent of introduction as well as certain conditions of habitat. Sometimes the infusion of one gene pool into another can be very small. In other cases, it can be so extensive as to obscure the genotype of the native species. Hybridization in cutthroat can sometimes be difficult to detect, at least to the naked eye. The variation in color and spotting in greenback is confusing enough, let alone the extensive variety of these same features in closely related subspecies such as Colorado River cutthroat and Yellowstone cutthroat. Hybridization with rainbows is probably easier to detect than hybridization with other cutthroat species. Rainbow-greenback hybrids may exhibit features of both species, including the red slashes and gills of a cutthroat as well as the red stripes of a rainbow. One way to determine the presence of rainbow hybridization in cutthroat is to examine the base of the tongue for tiny *basibranchial teeth*. A cutthroat possesses these little teeth on the top of its tongue, while rainbows generally do not.

Hybridization may reveal itself in other morphological features that differ either in number or in geometrical relation from the standard measurements of pure populations. Some of the meristic, or countable, characters that have been used to distinguish between species include gill-raker count, scale counts, and pyloric caeca count (that is, thin appendages on the intestine). Scientists may consider other meristic characters—such as the number of branchiostegal rays, the number of vertebrae, and the number of rays in the various fins—when differentiating between species.

In addition to traditional morphology, scientists have developed other methods to measure species purity. Today, geneticists can choose from a number of different biochemical techniques, including nuclear and mitochondrial

DNA testing. In theory, a look at chromosome complement, or *karyotype*, can help to distinguish between rainbows and cutthroat. Chromosome numbers for cutthroat vary from sixty-four to sixty-eight, while the numbers for rainbow typically run between fifty-eight and sixty. Scientists may also consider biogeography when distinguishing between species. Finally, stocking records can provide information on the historical introduction of nonnative species at specific sites. All of these strategies are presently used by managers to determine species purity for cutthroat in the West.

The day hikers have arrived. Another fisherman shows up. I've been warned in Todd Hosman's book, *Fly Fishing Rocky Mountain National Park*, that Loch Vale is one of the more popular lakes in the park, that on any given day a fly caster might find himself the subject of tourist photography. I've purposefully heeded the warning by proceeding to the far side of the lake, leaving the outlet for the other angler and his circle of admiring spectators. Looking back in amazement, I witness Hosman's prophecy unfold. The fisherman seems to relish the attention, willfully posing for the camera as he hauls in a trout. Looks like a classic case of life (the photographed fisherman) imitating art (Hosman's description) imitating life (the author's previous experience) itself imitated in art (the photo described in the book), which of course is imitating life (fly fishing), which to some is an art form based on the real-life urge to catch fish. And now, since I'm describing here how I *observed* the event, we can take it at least one step further and...well, you get the idea.

Turning away from the spectacle, I make my way around a small peninsula to the edge of a large protected cove. One thing about these trout: once you catch a fish in a certain area, the others get wise to it. What this means, of course, is that the first cast is critical—perhaps your best chance at getting a big fish. From the trees, I cast a dark caddis along the bank where submerged boulders provide shadowy cover. The fly turns over nicely as I wait, watching thistledown roll across the glassy surface until it catches on a strand of silk and stops dead in the water.

A large trout eases out of the shadows and takes the fly. Its white belly flashes in the green lake, twisting vertically. The fish wants to run for the rocks as I angle the rod to keep it in the open water. Eventually, I work it close enough to hold—a female from the looks of it, fourteen inches of fat trout. Excellent fish. I've brought my own camera today, thinking I should begin to document some of the trout I catch. In the process of getting the camera ready, the cutt flops across the dusty bank and plunks into the lake. A wisp of crooked monofilament dangles from the rod tip. She's broken the line, slipped away with the hook still lodged in her mouth. Alone on the bank I feel as though I've violated some basic trust, broken a covenant, all for a lousy photograph. I've heard that trout possess the wherewithal to eventually dislodge a hook on their own. Still, it's hardly enough to overcome my disappointment. We want things perfect in life. When they're not, and they rarely are, it's a feeling like death.

These are tough times for fishers. In this age of chronic self-consciousness, fly casters have become acutely aware of the criticisms directed their way. Today, the moral integrity of catch-and-release fishing is under attack, and with it, the self-esteem of fly casters everywhere. According to its detractors, catch-and-release amounts to the needless infliction of pain and stress on wild trout, all for the simple purpose of recreation. Stung by these charges of abuse, and unable to fully resolve the inherent contradictions in their sport, contemporary fly fishers have become mired in an ethical morass, paralyzed by doubt and deep pangs of conscience. It's true, fly fishing has become a purely symbolic activity for many of us, a ritual really, deriving most of its significance not from the procurement of food but rather in the reenactment of an ancient rite that seems to offer some spiritual or psychological reward. One only has to look at all the recent literature to see this. Sure, there are some "how-to" manuals still out there, but by and large, fly fishing has emerged as a touchstone for all kinds of meditations on sex, death, God, etc. Strip away all the metaphysical finery, the naysayers contend, and what you have is a classic game of dominance and control, sanctioned by a presumption of forgiveness implicit in the act of releasing trout "unharmed" back into the water.

It's all pretty confusing by now, but I think I started fishing as a boy because it was fun. If I remember right, I made the daily pilgrimage to that rank Ohio pond for the pure sake and pleasure of watching bluegill and sunfish charge a soaking worm. Later, when I started to harvest my catch, this too seemed perfectly natural since we always ate what we kept. Even after switching to a fly rod, it never occurred to me that I was doing anything wrong or immoral. On the contrary, it seemed that I was progressing as a citizen, becoming more conscientious in my approach to trout. Like most fly casters anymore, I practice a catch-and-release ethic that may sound foolish, pretentious, or responsible, depending on your particular point of view. But unethical? Abusive?

Few would deny that catch-and-release fly fishing is fraught with internal contradiction. We expend terrific amounts of time and energy in pursuit of an endangered game species with the expressed purpose of "freeing" the fish once we've subjected it to a measure of stress and pain, all the while believing that we're doing something good for it and ourselves. And although there certainly is an element of self-deception in this, we should not overlook the fundamental sense of responsibility at the core of the ethic. Yes, we all would like things perfect, but the fact is we don't live in a world of absolutes, and it seems just as misleading to ignore some of the broader issues of what's going on here, including whatever it is that fly fishers find so compelling about hunting trout. Which brings us back to this question of why do it at all. And here, I have to reject the hypothesis that we are all just a bunch of pathological control freaks. Hopeless, maybe. But malicious, no.

So, why do it? Why stand all day under a hot sun, fighting mosquitoes and treacherous moss-covered rocks, staring for hours at a tiny tuft of animal hair wrapped around a half-inch steel shank? What compels a grown adult to wade out in the snow and rain and lightning, all for a chance at a ten-inch trout he never intends to keep in the first place? (For that matter, why prod a pinkie inside the mouth of a cuttbow, just to feel around for a few tiny teeth?) Damned if he won't completely forget himself in the process, lose his head in the hunt, keep right on fishing well past dark, casting "by instinct," he'll say later with a straight face. To a casual observer, his behavior might seem excessive. Shameful. But the fact is, he can never get enough. There's always the next hole to fish, a different pattern to try, a new technique to practice, another stream or lake or flats to fish somewhere beyond the horizon. And what's *behind* this compulsion? What fuels his desire? Pure instinct, perhaps, but until geneticists provide the material proof, we are left with only questions and endless rhetoric—rhetoric, by the way, that can be refined and polished in those long intervals of idle contemplation while the better half of the brain busies itself with the mechanics of catching fish.

Ask fly fishers why they do what they do, and you're likely to get a variety of responses. They might tell you that fly fishing demands a special attention to natural conditions and that success depends not on conquest but rather on a skillful interaction with the elements of wind, water, light, and aquatic life. They might go further and explain that direct experience with the objects and creatures of the natural world clarifies our understanding of the unity of nature and our essential connection to the harmonies, rhythms, and cycles of life. Fishing, they'll say, evokes ancient mysteries and archetypal meanings. At this point, they might grow wistful and stare off in the distance as they try to describe how such a connection locates us in the universe and allows us to deal with the problem of impermanence. A different angler, probably a scientist, might direct you to the recent theories suggesting that humans have a genetically based emotional need to affiliate with the natural world. As the brain evolved in a biocentric world, survival and well-being depended on how effectively individuals coped with the natural environment. Accordingly, natural selection favored those who displayed a genetic tendency to learn the appropriate responses to lethal threats, desirable habitats, rising trout. If he is Scottish and Presbyterian and can write like the dickens, another angler might tell you that all good things, trout as well as eternal salvation, come by grace and grace comes by art and art is performed on a four-count rhythm between ten and two o'clock. Still another fisher might get mystical on you and explain that in our participation of the hunt, we engage in a pure state of being in which subject and object merge. Acting on a most fundamental instinct of predation, we manifest our own wildness and in the process allow for some kind of personal recovery.

But if I really had to say myself, I might begin by looking at the various phases I've passed through as a fisherman. What began as a pastime evolved into a means to secure food, later a hobby, and only now as a loose form of meditation. The reasons I fish today have more to do with intangible considerations than anything else. Yes, I like the fight. The bigger the better. I enjoy the challenge of trying to deceive trout, the sense of quest it affords, the surge of adrenaline when a fish strikes, the pleasure of seeing myself react automatically. But like I say, it all gets pretty confusing and if I had to be honest, if I really had to say what attracts me most about fly fishing, all I could probably ever be sure of is that it gets me into beautiful places with something nearly as beautiful to do.

At the end of the day, I return to the peninsula by the cove and prop myself against a rock in the shade of a small wind-twisted spruce. The day hikers are all gone now, headed back down the trail. To the west, the mountain ridges recede in gradations of smoky blue—the more distant the mountain, the lighter the color. Shadows from the Divide fall across the headwall and snow-patched cirque. A nearby snag stands in stark contrast to the craggy peaks behind it, its weathered trunk scored with spiral lines. Look carefully, I think to myself. Remember what you see.

A trout roils the surface, starting a flash of sparkling gems across the water. I can see the red gill flap and belly, the dark spots and green back as it swims through the lake. Memory tells me that fish are in fact bigger than what they appear to be underwater. Along the bank, reflected sunlight plays upon the undersides of a fir bough. A strand of cobweb extends from the end of the branch to some point along the bank that I cannot see, reflecting an inch or two of fine, narrow sunlight. If I disregard memory and forget what I've learned, I see a single filament of light hovering by itself over the water.

Look carefully, I think again.

Trout are feeding everywhere now on both sides of the peninsula. An image of Taylor Glacier appears on the surface as an impressionistic tableau superimposed on a topography of lake bottom. In the deeper water, the top half of a giant boulder rises out of the green depths, not far from a submerged branch that I mistook earlier for a trout swimming to my fly. In that moment of expectation, a myriad of impressions raced through my mind: a sudden birdcall taken as an omen, a shift in the wind, indications of an emerging hatch…so much condensed in a single moment. And in that instant when a trout really does rise to a fly, the world comes to a stop, poised for what's to happen next.

Don't ever forget.

Sitting under the cover of this solitary tree, watching and listening as scores of greenback cruise around me in golden sunlight, I can't help but feel that I'm witnessing a moment of perfection. Eternity in a drop of time. I am here, conscious of my surroundings, keenly aware. Alert. Indeed, part of the scene.

COMO CREEK (8,900'), EARLY OCTOBER

By the early part of the century, the effects of competition and hybridization had decimated cutthroat populations all across the West. Cutthroats of the interior basins seemed especially vulnerable. In the decades that followed, hybridization would complicate efforts to restore native cutthroats to their original habitats. Although there had been some attempt to reestablish the greenback in its native range as early as 1959, these efforts were frustrated by the lack of a pure-strain population that could serve as a brood stock. That all changed in 1969 when Dr. Behnke confirmed the existence of pure-strain greenbacks in a small tributary called Como Creek.

You might expect it to be fairly easy to locate a stream in your home county, even if it is a small tributary. At least this is what I thought. But when the creek doesn't show up on local maps and the Forest Service can't find it either, then you either give up hope or wait for a serious stroke of serendipity. Which is what I got down at the county courthouse, waiting in line to settle a small legal matter. Hanging on the wall behind the counter was a large replica map of the county, showing a tributary stream in the mountains named Como Creek. I took note of its shape and direction and later located the area on my own map where it ought to be. According to my topo, Como was the biggest tributary feeding North Boulder Creek from the north, just west of the Peak-to-Peak Highway.

I guess right, after all. Situated along the eastern slopes of Niwot Ridge and Arapahoe Morain, Como Creek flows in a southeasterly direction down to its confluence with North Boulder Creek. My hunch is confirmed by an old rusted sign along a washed-out two-track in the trees off the highway, a sign riddled with bullet holes that reads: "Como Cr k Closed to Fis ing Due To Protec on of Gre ack Cut roat."

I follow a path down to the creek, through an aspen grove and meadow golden in autumn sunlight. The aspens are thick and tough as wrought iron. I study the calligraphy of knots scripted on the bark, how they resemble big soulful eyes. The older the tree, it seems, the more profound the expression. In this forest of eyes, Como Creek spans three feet across at most, its water slightly tannic. Air bubbles drift through the current, casting round shadows on the creek bed. The ripples in the current make shadows of their own, fine black ribs weaving across the bottom.

And so this is where the recovery begins. This is the brink of extinction.

In 1952, a University of Colorado graduate student named Bill Rickard caught a few cutthroat outside his cabin at the university's Science Lodge where he was working for the summer. An accomplished fly fisherman, Rickard noticed that the trout looked different from any he had ever seen. Suspecting that he may have discovered a population of the "extinct" greenback, the young scientist sent specimens to Dr. Howard Tanner of Colorado State University, who then forwarded them to the National Museum of Natural History in Washington, D.C. The museum reported a positive match with its own "type-specimen" greenback. A natural barrier had apparently prevented brook trout from migrating up the creek where Rickard fished, thus preserving the genetic purity of this isolated population.

It would be seventeen years before Behnke officially confirmed the existence of pure-strain greenbacks in Como Creek. Scientists promptly removed sixty of the fish and planted fifty-two of them at Black Hollow near Fort Collins to expand the range. The following year, Behnke identified what he believed to be a second pure population along the headwaters of the South Fork of the Cache la Poudre River. In 1977, a third population of pure-strain greenbacks was reportedly found in Cascade Creek, a small tributary of the South Huerfano River in the Arkansas River drainage. There would be other reported discoveries of relict greenback populations in the years ahead.

A small trout darts for the shadows. Yellow aspen leaves whirl in the current, spinning through the riffles like gold dollars. Grasshoppers cackle in the meadow, and so I chase one down—offer it in the creek. A greenback rises from below the bank and takes it off the surface. I return to the meadow to look for another hopper, as a warm breeze stirs the quaking aspens. The sun, angled low on its way to the arc of winter equinox, bathes the aspen grove in a luminous golden light. The sun, whose light takes eight minutes to reach the earth, shines in a perfect blue sky. A ridge of high pressure dominates the mountain West today, stalling a storm system bearing down from the Northwest—a system created from wind and sea currents in the North Pacific. For those of us on the ground, it is simply Indian summer.

And exactly what do I expect to find here along this creek, too small to warrant a name on local maps? Here in the county I call home, as I look to find my own place in the world through a connection I can make with the land? Like the last of the great herds of wild bison reduced to a mere twenty-three animals in the Yellowstone backcountry, the greenback found refuge here at Como Creek. Caught at this particular crossroads of history—a century removed from the slaughter of bison, the gold rushes, and Indian wars—do I seek my own refuge? In the last fragments of wildness, do I look for my own recovery?

I catch a second grasshopper in the meadow and toss it into a lower pool, not altogether certain why or what I expect to get out of this, except that it feels right. But is it the response of trout that I find pleasing, or my own participation in the process? Some affinity with the animal world, or simply my ability to replicate a natural accident? The old doubts crowd in. Surely, I could trace all of this to some personal deficiency, some chronic sense of dissociation in a world that seems to be coming apart at the seams. How does one ever get beyond his own personal desires, anyway? Worse, this gesture resonates with a sense of loss, a personal as well as collective loss over what is happening to the planet. It's like I'm trying to recover some innocence here that was never mine, that perhaps never even existed.

Aw hell, I think. I'm only tossing a few grasshoppers into the creek.

Speaking of which, there goes one now flying through the meadow. I trap the hopper in the grass and drop it in a braid of current funneling between the banks, watching as the hopper gains speed, drifts and whirls where the stream unravels in a quiet pool. A greenback snatches it off the surface, starting a ring across the water. The trout seems to be aware of my presence as it returns to the edge of the bank. I can see the red blush around the gill, the crimson under the belly, the spots along the tail, the black eye.

And what are you thinking, small fish? Pray tell, what lies at the heart of your awareness of me? Watching the greenback watch me, I imagine the both of us cautious and alert, each cognizant of the mysterious *other*. Molded from the same ground, he to swim and I to walk, we watch together. Bodies of clay, eyes of earth. It is this awareness that we share, under a common star whose light takes all of eight minutes to arrive.

Hidden Valley Beaver Ponds (9,200'), Mid-October

Call it curiosity or just plain human contrariness, but on a clear day late in the season I decide to visit Lily Lake, a popular roadside fishing destination. Lily comes complete with parking lot, groomed trails, picnic facilities…in short, all the signs of high-pressure fishing. By early morning, a number of bellyboaters are already on the water, as well as a half-dozen fishermen wading from shore. I've heard that spawning season can get ugly here—fishermen intentionally foul hooking greenback in shallow water, that sort of thing. A real bloodbath, according to one friend who refuses to fish here anymore. "For ethical reasons," he explains. Like him, I tend to view fishing as a solitary endeavor—a chance to forget one's social preoccupations in the sound of running water, the play of light and shadow, the whims of wild trout. In the presence of other anglers, a fisherman's pride can often get the best of him. It's not so much that he has to beat the other guy as that he hates to lose. This is true not only in fishing but in other important pursuits like poker, eight ball, and puck glide. There's probably a lesson somewhere in all of this, though I'd be the last to know.

On my way around the lake I pass a fly fisher outfitted in army fatigues, neoprene chest waders, side-lens glasses. He's fishing leeches, he allows, with moderate success. I continue on to the far end of the lake and what is clearly the least-desirable place to fish. It's shallow and muddy and full of weeds, but at least I'll be alone here. I assemble the rod as two hikers pass on the cinder trail behind me, discussing stocks and the national labor pool. Another passerby speaks loudly into a cell phone. Distracted now, I can't decide what fly to use. But it hardly seems to matter. Sometimes a soul just *knows* he's not going to catch anything.

Time to readjust. Take a step back. I tie on a dark caddis and watch for a while. A single cutthroat cruises the shoreline, drifting in three feet of water just off the bank. I cast the fly, but the trout passes without so much as a nod. Ten minutes later, another cutthroat appears and again I put the caddis close. Same result. Either these are supremely ignorant greenback, or their nonchalance borders on arrogance. More likely, they've seen so much hardware and feather that they're more than a little wise to it all. I'll just have to be patient, sight cast, and take my chances on a good presentation.

Another greenback swims by *very* slowly, twenty feet offshore, pausing in the shadow of a large boulder. When he moves away I twitch the fly slightly, catching his attention. I can see the white of his lower lip as he rises to the caddis. He doesn't take it, but at least this one has reacted. A second trout now appears from the left, as the bigger greenback returns to chase off the newcomer. One quick false cast to whip dry the fly, and I put the caddis on his nose. This time he strikes.

When I get it close to the bank the big cutt thrashes at the surface, twisting and turning, churning a muddy froth. By the time I free the hook and place him back in the lake, weave water across the gills and watch him swim away, the bellyboaters and spincasters have taken notice. Anxious for a piece of the action, a half-dozen anglers casually move down the lake and crowd in around me like, well, leeches. Bellyboaters invade from offshore, whipping flyline over my casting range. A lure flies off a spinning reel and splashes ten yards away. Etiquette now, boys. Dammit, don't crowd me in. Don't you know I'm serious at this stuff? Dyed-in-the-wool and tested true? Why, I've been all through these hills for greenback, damn near lost a toe in the snow. So, how about a little *respect*?

But all is fair in love and war and high-pressure fishing, so they say. Or should have said. Demographers inform us that the global rate of human population growth is diminishing. Still, the number of people in the world is increasing, right? The encounter at Lily Lake proves civil in the end. We do not cut each other's lines, throw rocks, exchange blows or epithets or even dirty looks. Rather, we play out our little dance of common courtesy, finding the steps as we go. But for me, the incident comes as a reminder of my own lack of social graces when it comes to crowds, or, more precisely, *crowding*. In time, the other anglers depart the weedy end of Lily, and by early afternoon, most will have left the lake altogether. By then, I will have moved into the broken shadows at the back corner of the lake where I'll wait for large trout to happen by, watching as they rise to the surface without so much as a wave of tail or fin. But as big and beautiful as these greenbacks are, perhaps the biggest on average of anywhere, I too depart Lily Lake. For a place in the park where I know I'll be alone.

*   *   *

It's been twenty years since I first came to the mountains to fish for western cutthroat. A notice in the local newspaper announced the opening of a limited season on greenbacks in Rocky Mountain National Park, and I knew right away this was something I should do. I was new to the West, and this seemed like a good way to get acclimated. In fact, what I remember most about those early years was the clear sense of purpose I brought to the mountains. Of course, a lot has happened since then. A lot of trout and a lot of trouble. So much of the latter, in fact, that if I didn't know any better, I'd say that the losses accrued in these years alone would be enough to last a lifetime. If once, long ago, I stood among the wildflowers in Chautauqua Meadow and wondered what changes were in store for me, the years would provide the answer.

Rosemarie and I married, eventually, and bought a house together. Things seemed to be falling into place for us. While finishing graduate school, I played in a rock band long enough to think I might even have a career in music. I could see my life unfolding before me, taking shape as it entered this new phase, and I welcomed the changes. But this new life didn't last, and soon all of it was gone—marriage, house, band. The succession of losses caught me off guard. Thinking a fresh start might be in order, I accepted a teaching position in North Carolina, only to resign after a year to return to Colorado. I missed the Rocky Mountains more than I could know. Then, on a sunny day in late summer, I found myself back at the front door of cabin 506.

So these are the losses, the changes in store.

But that's the way it goes. Let's face it, the times we live in aren't exactly conducive to continuity. The American fetish to break from the past and start anew, to get while the gettin's good, seems to be as infectious as ever. We make choices based on circumstances as we see them, for reasons that make sense at the time. We do the best we can. Along the way, maybe we discover a few things. Maybe we learn that compromise is convenient, if not exactly necessary—that honesty has a price, trust can be leveraged, allegiances are negotiable. And if in the end there remains anything of value, why, we'll be sure to notice when it comes time to add it all up.

I don't remember much about that first trip to the Beaver Ponds, only that I was alone and caught fish, about half as many brook trout as greenback. I did not encounter another angler that day, nor would I in the ensuing years. This has always surprised me a bit, inasmuch as the ponds are located along a paved road inside one of America's most popular national parks. Moreover, the Park Service has constructed a boardwalk across a number of the ponds and intervening waterways, providing easy access for anyone to view the meadow close up. The fishing at the Beaver Ponds is okay, nothing spectacular. The greenbacks tend to be of average size and the scenery is fine, though nothing like it is elsewhere in the park. So, it wasn't for these reasons that I came back to fish the ponds the following year. Though I couldn't have known then what only later would become clear, I found myself returning to the Beaver Ponds every autumn to fish the same places with the same fly pattern for what must surely have been in some years the same trout. Only with time would I come to understand that what draws me here is precisely this idea of *return*: to mark the seasons, renew old acquaintances, to add another ring on the tree of memory.

The Beaver Ponds, located in Hidden Valley beneath a long flat of upland tundra known as Trail Ridge, became one of the first reintroduction sites for greenbacks. When the U.S. Endangered Species Act was passed in 1973, the greenback cutthroat was immediately classified as an endangered species. Three years later, the State of Colorado added the greenback to its own list of endangered species. This prompted a coordinated restoration effort involving a number of state and federal agencies, including the Colorado Division of Wildlife, U.S. Fish and Wildlife Service, National Park Service, and U.S. Forest Service. With greenbacks it captured from Como Creek in 1977, the Greenback Cutthroat Recovery Team established a hatchery brood stock at the Federal Fish Culture Development Center in Bozeman, Montana. In addition to its spawning efforts, the Recovery Team was also busy preparing a suitable habitat for the greenback's return. Chemical poisons were used in some cases to eradicate nonnative species, especially brook trout. Fish barriers were constructed to prevent upstream migration into lakes designated for reintroduction.

Beginning in 1981, biologists transplanted fry and fingerlings from the Bozeman hatchery into several lakes and streams in Rocky Mountain National Park and adjacent Roosevelt National Forest. The following year, the Hidden Valley Beaver Ponds were opened for catch-and-release fishing. Between

1982 and 1986, other alpine lakes and streams became available for restricted fishing including Lily Lake, Fern Lake, and Ouzel Lake. In 1986, efforts got under way to restore greenbacks to select streams and lakes in the Arkansas River drainage. In the years since, the recovery of greenback cutthroat has come to be regarded nationally as a major success story in the field of conservation. Today, greenbacks are thought to be present in sixty-two different sites, forty-seven of which are open to catch-and-release fishing.

Fly fishers have played a helpful role in the recovery process. In 1978, the Recovery Team downlisted the status of greenback cutthroat from endangered to threatened, paving the way for catch-and-release fishing. Anglers were encouraged to harvest brook trout from such places as Hidden Valley in an attempt to improve conditions for greenback. This kind of participation generated public interest in native cutthroat and created a constituency to help support recovery efforts. Since the 1980s, Trout Unlimited has been actively involved in the restoration of greenbacks, providing money as well as manpower to a host of recovery projects. In fact, the collaboration between greenback managers and fishermen has often been cited around the country as a key ecological argument for catch-and-release fishing.

Efforts to restore greenbacks to their native range are ongoing. As genetic testing improves and new findings emerge, program managers continue to adjust their strategies to the best available science. A recent study conducted at the University of Colorado suggests that five out of nine putatively relict greenback populations may in fact be composed of Colorado River cutthroat or a hybrid form. Although further testing is expected, the implications of this latest study are far-reaching. Because a number of these relict populations have been used in the past as brood stocks, it's conceivable that some restoration populations may be more hybridized than previously thought. Given the widespread stocking of nonnative species that has occurred since the late nineteenth century, it's no surprise that efforts to restore native cutthroat should encounter such complications. In fact, by the time scientists even began a systematic study of the greenback in the 1880s, extensive stocking of Yellowstone cutthroat and Colorado River cutthroat had already taken place in Front Range waters.

There are places to fish along the ponds that I have come to count on over the years: the beaver dam, the bank beside the willow thicket, the hill on the far side. I can see them now in my mind, as I search for the words to describe exactly what this place means. I purposely saved the Beaver Ponds for last, partly because I'm in the habit of visiting here late in the year, but also because I wanted to see if anything would be different after fishing so many other lakes. But the truth is, I really don't have much to say. Nothing, anyway, that seems especially worthwhile. All the science and history and hiking and fishing just seem to run together. All of it fades into a casual afterthought, until it's late in the day and I am crossing the dam to reach the hill along the far bank.

Once across, I climb high enough to gain a good view of the near flat in shadows. A bull elk has moved onto the ridge above me, as the sun sinks low in the cleft of the valley. For the better part of the afternoon, the forest has been ringing with the sound of bugling elk. Now, the song of this one lone animal soars in the gathering twilight. Soon, a beaver will begin its nightly rounds on the lower pond, punctuating each dive with a thunderous whack! By then, most of the elk will have moved out of the trees into the open draws of Horseshoe Park.

From the hill, I watch as three greenback approach from the left—drifting slowly along the shallow flats, cruising the bottom for food. I blow the wings dry on a Royal Coachman and follow their progress. The trout move out of the shadows into the deeper water, where the pond catches the last of the day's sunlight. Shards of blue and green and bronze weave across the water.

A breeze passes over the surface when I think I see a flash of gold in the dance of wind and water, sky and earth.

8. *Ice Out*

It's hot, today. Triple-digit hot. Too damn hot.

So I take to the hills, to gain some elevation and escape this godforsaken swelter that comes at you like the fiery breath of a furnace. I'll get away for a few nights to the high country and a place I've wanted to see for some time now on account of its big valley, backcountry fishing, and the glaciers—six at last count—that grace the eastern slope of the Divide along the headwaters of the Middle St. Vrain Creek. But there's another reason now to go, more pressing and ominous, that also has to do with the heat. The glaciers are vanishing—here and everywhere around the world. As the planet continues to warm, nearly all the world's alpine glaciers could disappear by the end of the century. Here in Colorado, glaciers that have existed for hundreds of years could all be gone within a few decades.

It's been raining off and on the past few days, but now the colors of the valley shine in the sun: purple and scarlet wildflowers, a deep-blue sky, patches of snow along the verdant tundra. Shouldering my pack, rod case in hand, I cross a wooden bridge at the trailhead that spans the raucous creek. I'll follow the trail along the Middle Fork all the way to the head of Peaceful Valley, one of many alpine drainages running east along the Front Range. Sculpted by glaciers during the last ice age, this classic U-shaped valley is framed on both sides by high, treeless ridges.

At ten thousand feet, the trail enters a forest of spruce and fir, where shafts of luminous sunlight pour through the canopy. Even at this altitude I can feel the heat, and so I tend toward the shade, sipping water from the hose tucked beneath a shoulder strap. I pass deadfall and large boulders covered in green and silver lichen. This is home ground. All very familiar. It is reassuring to know on a day like this that this backcountry is here. That I can hike ten miles to the Continental Divide and expect to be alone. That there are glaciers where I'm going.

An older couple is walking my way on the trail. The man carries a large wooden basket. He is originally from Russia, I learn, and she from the Ukraine. They are out today harvesting mushrooms, a hobby acquired in the Old Country. The man shows me a large *Boletus* mushroom at the bottom of his basket, cradled in a paper towel stained yellow and orange. There are other kinds of mushrooms in this valley that hunters covet, including *Cantharellus* and *Pleurotus*. While July is a good time for *Boletus*, the collecting is better "upstairs," the man tells me, pointing to higher ground.

About three miles from the trailhead, I come into Coney Flats—an open park situated at the confluence where Coney Creek drains into the valley from the south. The flats are composed of material washed from the front of a retreating glacier that stood long enough to build a small recessional moraine. The open meadows offer broad views of the high peaks and ridges enclosing the valley. To the south is Buchanan Pass, hard by the summit of Sawtooth Mountain, where the Divide begins to turn west toward the glaciers and cirques of the headwaters. Sawtooth marks the easternmost approach of the Continental Divide in all of North America. On the other side of the valley—nearly two thousand feet high—a rock wall rises to the high peaks of Elk Tooth and Ogalalla, separating Peaceful Valley from Wild Basin and marking the boundary between the Indian Peaks Wilderness and Rocky Mountain National Park.

The meadows shimmer with wildflowers—Indian paintbrush, larkspur, columbine, golden aster, purple daisies, lupine, harebells, arnica, wild rose. Butterflies flash in sunlight: a painted lady that will later migrate onto the plains when the weather turns, a mourning cloak fanning its wings on a log. Whites and blues gather in clumps along the damp sand of the trail, some with eyespots and pretty papier-mâché wings. Meanwhile, the creek, slightly tannic in the bright sun, rushes past in whitewater and falls. In a hurry, it seems, for its rendezvous with the South Platte on the plains.

Leaving Coney Flats, I begin a climb through trees where a number of trails converge near the entrance to the wilderness. I continue on, watching the white rump of a flicker as it flies ahead. A dark-eyed junco whirls in the trees, its forked tail gleaming in the sun.

But it's hot, and after a mile or two I stop to rest, choosing a shady spot near a clearing where I can lean against a broad stump and get some water for the aching soreness in my throat. Let my feet and back relax. Try to cool down some.

At the hottest part of the day along this particular stretch of trail, there's no wind or birdsong, no humming of insects. Everything seems to stand still in the heat. I can almost hear the ground baking in the sun. Down at lower elevations, the plains must surely be scorching. In fact, it's shaping up to be one of the planet's warmest years on record, approaching the all-time high set only a year ago.

After enjoying a relatively stable climate for thousands of years, the earth is heating up. For centuries, man has been pouring carbon dioxide and other heat-trapping gases into the atmosphere faster than plants and oceans can absorb them. Over the past 140 years, atmospheric CO_2 has increased by 33 percent, making today's levels the highest of any in at least 650,000 years. As CO_2 levels continue to rise, so too should the heat. Global temperatures, up by more than one degree Fahrenheit over the past century, are expected to rise an additional three and a half to eight degrees in the coming century.

Not surprisingly, the world's ice is in retreat everywhere—from the great ice sheets of Antarctica and Greenland to the Arctic sea ice and the permafrost of Alaska and Siberia. Mountain and valley glaciers seem especially vulnerable. Since the late nineteenth century, alpine glaciers have been in an overall decline on every continent of the world. In that time, the total surface area of glaciers has decreased by 50 percent. Glaciers in the Tibetan Plateau are retreating so fast that researchers believe that most central and eastern Himalayan glaciers could virtually disappear by 2035. In the Alps, glaciers will all but vanish by 2050, if not sooner. The snows that have covered Mount Kilimanjaro for eleven thousand years could all be gone within a decade.

Here in western North America, it's the same story. All forty-seven North Cascade glaciers are retreating. In the Waterton-Glacier park complex on the U.S.-Canada border, several major glaciers have shrunk by 50 percent or more in recent decades. On the U.S. side, the number of glaciers in Glacier National Park has dropped from 150 in 1850 to fewer than 30 today, and most of those remaining have diminished in size by two-thirds. Within thirty years, it is predicted, most if not all of the park's namesake glaciers will disappear.

I continue through the trees, rising gradually into a subalpine world. Common juniper and mountain blueberry grow in the clearings. Kinnikinnick, too. A blue sheen colors the standing water in pockets of mud.

Up ahead, three workers from the Forest Service are spraying plants along the side of the trail. I stop to say hello to the woman wearing a floppy shade hat and the two young men she's supervising. She says they're trying to eradicate toadflax and Canada thistle—two invasive species that have found a new home here. When I mention I am on my way to the glacier, she shakes her head and tells me it's "a shadow of its former self."

Higher up, only a few miles from the head of the valley, I come into a clearing where a pile of weathered boards stands next to a tumbledown shack— the remains of a logging operation back in the fifties. Ranchers first began to settle Peaceful Valley, then called Wildcat Gulch, as early as 1883. Although it's been a half century since loggers were here, evidence of their activities is plain to see. For the past few miles of the hike, I've passed broad stumps of enormous trees that have been felled. The open meadows of Coney Flats are what they are today as a result of clear-cutting.

That the extractive industries of logging and grazing and mining have done a number on western landscape shouldn't come as a complete surprise. After all, commerce was the driving force behind western expansion right from the outset. Even before the discovery of gold in Colorado in 1859, Americans were looking to cash in on what was here. In fact, St. Vrain Creek takes its name from a French-born trapper, Ceran St. Vrain, who in 1837 teamed with the Bent brothers to build a trading post not far from where the river empties into the South Platte. In addition to outfitting mountain men, Fort St. Vrain was in the business of trading trinkets and beads to the Arapaho and Cheyenne for buffalo hides and tongues.

All of which gets me to thinking about place-names. As in other parts of the West, many of the prominent geographic features along the Front Range bear the names of American businessmen, soldiers, and politicians.

But not all.

Across the Divide from here is Hell Canyon. Next to that is Paradise Park. Inside Paradise is a reserve where camping is prohibited. In this "forbidden area" of Paradise, National Park officials seek to preserve the ecosystem in its natural state in order to maintain an ecological baseline against which future changes might be measured. Rumor has it, there are lakes nearby that hold giant stockers—trout that were introduced years ago that have since grown to enormous size. As recently as a decade ago, these lunkers reportedly lived in remote lakes, unable to reproduce. Just grow big. Although I have no intention of crossing the Divide to enter Paradise, I must say, as an angler, the temptation to venture into the forbidden area is considerable.

Paradise. Forbidden area. Hell. The allusions are too obvious to ignore. The fabled fruit of knowledge is alive and well here in the Colorado mountains. That the names should insinuate the backcountry as something otherworldly strikes me as a bit curious. Bizarre, even.

But it's all a ruse, it seems to me. All just a grandiose distraction. The fact is, we've excused all gods from the equation. Today, *we* play God. Think Kurtz, Raskolnikov, Dr. Moreau. What gets lost in the process is any sense of circumspection, any serious consideration of the consequences of our actions. And here we are, poised to reach deeper into Pandora's box, rushing headlong into new and future technologies of bioengineering, cloning, nanotechnology—with little regard for what unforeseen surprises such tinkering will bring.

As if we didn't have our hands full already.

I've lost my way. Somewhere I strayed from the trail, and now I find myself at the edge of the creek, facing a large boulder field with no clear way to proceed. If I stay on this side of the creek, I'll have to pick my way through the talus. Not the best option, it seems. Footing will be an issue, and besides, the heat has left me tired. Groggy. Better to stay on level ground if possible. The creek, meanwhile, offers no plausible crossing. The torrent of icy water, with its noisy rapids and swift current, seems impassable.

So I keep walking, staying close to the creek, until I come to a logjam where the water backs up a bit. Leaning against the push of current, using my rod case for balance, I start across. Soon I'm up to my waist in frigid runoff, careful to position my feet solidly along the bottom, cognizant of my balance and the pressure against my thighs. In the midst of this cold flow of snow-melt, this pulse of water and gravity, my sixty-pound pack has a mind of its own. Top heavy and whimsical. Mustn't slip or lose balance, else I bash the logs.

Alone in the backcountry, one learns to be cautious. Especially if the heat has gone to one's head. Never underestimate the power of natural forces. Disaster happens fast, often unannounced.

Once across, I find a footpath and continue upstream to a fallen tree that spans the rushing creek. Finding my balance on its skinned bulk, I gingerly step across to the other side where yellow cinquefoil blooms along the bank.

A mile farther, the trail rises to a massive logjam at the edge of a shallow pond. Looking through the trees, I see other ponds along the valley floor. Traversing the logs, careful not to walk on any floaters, I find a path and follow it into a meadow, looking for a campsite somewhere among the many water-ways that wind through the valley. On a grassy peninsula separating the two biggest ponds, I pitch my tent and slather on bug juice, then go about assembling the rod—cinching down the reel, threading line through guides. Quick now, I tie on an attractor and walk down to the water.

I'll spend what remains of the day working the ponds and streams that run through the valley, catching cutthroat on dries. Casting onto a reflection of valley walls, I let the fly drift. Watch it bob in the wavelets when a breeze ruf-fles the surface. An ouzel dips at the edge of the water.

And when the sun veers for the serrated ridge in the west, the air be-comes radiant in golden light. Framed by towering scarps and peaks, the val-ley assumes the hallowed calm of a cathedral. The light mellows to amber, the clouds blush pink. A star appears overhead.

And still I fish on.

Like a kid, I creep through deadfall and shrub down to a bank near the in-let, peering over the edge to see a half-dozen cutthroat holding in the current. Pulling back, I drop a fly at the head of the rill and let it run down, hoping that a fish might be moved enough to react.

How fortunate I am to be here. To experience these timeless rhythms of running water, hatching insects, feeding trout. Rhythms that have played out over the eons, tuned to ancient cycles. Rhythms whose every moment is unique.

The glaciers have played a role in all of this. Here, as in other parts of the world, glaciers help to regulate stream flows year-round. In years of heavy precipitation, the snowpack protects glaciers from melting, keeping water high on the mountains. In warmer and drier years, the melting of glaciers increases, providing greater amounts of water to streams. By regulating flows, glaciers help to maintain the conditions by which species like cutthroat can survive. In the coming years, springtime snowpack is expected to diminish along the Front Range due to increased warming. As the glaciers shrink and in many cases disappear, so too will the amount of late-season runoff.

It's a strange feeling to witness the world at this crossroads. Any sense of wonder I have tonight is tempered by the realization that this ecosystem may be imperiled. Try as I might, it's difficult to fully grasp the large-scale changes that scientists say are afoot—difficult to imagine the planet as being anything other than what I have known in my forty-odd years. Such a strange conundrum: to behold so many marvels of nature, thousands of years in the making, fully aware that I may be witnessing their slow demise. In fact, having a hand in it. Tonight, under the stars of Paradise, it seems hard to believe.

At dawn, steam rises from the glassy pond. Across the misty water a large buck raises his head of antlers, then lowers it again to drink along the bank. A water bird scurries along the sandy flat.

I ready the waist pack: water, food, camera, and the rest. The idea is to spend the day above timberline, visiting the glaciers before returning to camp by nightfall.

All set to go, I start across the meadow for the footpath winding through the trees. In this ecotone between forest and tundra, the trail rises past marsh marigolds and snowfields. Snowmelt trickles across the muddy path. Insects are out and about this sunny morning, doing what they do in the way of pollination and recycling, providing the indispensable services without which this community of life could not survive.

Climbing steadily now to tundra, wending my way around slabs of granite, I'm greeted by a string of sharp, staccato barks. Marmot, I think to myself, pausing to locate its position. Peering through branches of krumholz, I catch a glimpse of its furry hide, perched on a rock where it announces my passing. I see pikas too, darting across boulders, entirely at home in this austere environment.

Rugged and roadless, this wilderness maintains a sense of the wild. The presence of man is minimized by the fact that a long hike is required to get here, the elevation is eleven thousand feet, and no valuable resource exists that can be feasibly extracted. Although it may appear to the naked eye that our impact is negligible, the Colorado high country remains vulnerable to acid rain and invasive species. And now, looming on the horizon, climate change threatens to disrupt the structure and dynamics of its ecological relations.

Any plant or animal species living at higher elevations is likely to be affected by future warming. Alpine species seem especially vulnerable. If timberline creeps higher in the coming decades, as many believe, alpine meadows will shrink and disappear. Whole communities of native plants will be displaced. Local bird species that depend on tundra—the white-tailed ptarmigan, American pipit, and rosy finches—could see their habitats vanish by the end of the century. Pikas, already in decline throughout the West, will continue to lose the lower limits of their range. With less snowpack and ice, runoff could decrease to the point where some streams are no longer able to support trout that depend on minimum flows of cold water. Frogs and bats and butterflies also stand to be affected by climate change. Pine beetle populations, a threat to forests across the West, should expand even further with warmer temperatures.

I climb higher, rising above timberline as a stream of meltwater rushes past. Wildflowers wave in the wind—yellow avens, fuchsia primrose, pink and white moss campion. From here I can see the southernmost glaciers, a patchwork of snowfields along the rocky slope of the cirque. To the east, a green shroud of forest descends into the valley. And to the north, a turquoise tarn glitters beneath the jagged peaks of Elk Tooth and Ogallala.

A rugged and raw place, this. Composed of scarps and scree, tundra and wildflower, ice and sky. Acres of jumbled granite in every conceivable configuration.

The sun plays hide-and-seek with restless clouds skirting the Divide. When it shines unabated, I feel its fierce rays on the exposed skin of my arms. Dense thickets of willow grow in the draw where runoff purls deep between boulders. In the distance, the sound of rushing water blends with the sough of wind.

Scrambling up the last ascent, I approach a tarn that sits in a catch basin below three glaciers. All three are modest in size, more like pockets of snow settled in the couloirs and depressions of the scree. One, called New Glacier, lies at the bottom of a long avalanche chute that drops twelve hundred feet from the Divide.

Before coming to Peaceful Valley, I tracked down old photographs of these glaciers taken in the early twentieth century. I've brought along a copy of one photo of New Glacier, dated September 1919. After studying its composition and vantage point, I scramble across a boulder field to find the spot where the photo was taken. I open the lens on my camera, adjust the zoom to match the old photo, and snap a half-dozen pictures. Compared to what they looked like in 1919, all three glaciers appear smaller today, especially the one directly to the east of New that has retreated significantly up the slope.

The biggest of the St. Vrain Glaciers, North and South, both lie a mile to the west. I have photographic images of them as well, taken in 1924 by Clint O. Dumm. When I'm done here, I'll hike to a rocky perch above North St. Vrain where I'll repeat the process, photographing both glaciers, discovering that they too appear smaller than what they were nearly a century ago. In one of the 1924 photos, the terminal of North towers thirty feet high. In another, South St. Vrain spans the entire breadth of its cirque, reaching in some places all the way to the ridge. The glacier today looks half this size, retreated to an elevation significantly lower on the wall.

First, though, I return to the tarn below New Glacier for a closer look. From the edge of the water, the three glaciers before me look anything but imposing. Rather, they seem fragile. Vulnerable. A thin veneer of melting snow covers the surface of polished ice. Where the ice is exposed, the darker gray color absorbs more heat. The glaciers are streaked with grit, and snow alga lends a faint hue of burgundy. At the center of one, a patch of bare ice shows through the snow. I look into the hole of ice, like a window into time.

A glimpse into the distant past.

The St. Vrain Glaciers were originally formed during the Little Ice Age, an episode of cooling that began in the thirteenth century and extended into the middle of the nineteenth century. The Little Ice Age represents the last of three small glacial advances that have occurred since the end of the Ice Age nearly twelve thousand years ago. During the final stage of the Ice Age, which peaked about twenty thousand years ago, glaciers up to thirteen thousand feet thick covered large areas of Alaska, most of Canada, all of New England, and much of the upper Midwest and northern Rockies. Here in Colorado, ice accumulated in most of the higher mountain ranges, including many east-facing valleys along the Front Range. Glaciers pushed their way down from the high mountains to elevations as low as eight thousand feet, eroding the sides of the valleys to give them their present U-shaped character.

Today, more than 135 permanent snow or ice bodies remain in Colorado, though only 14 of these have been officially named as glaciers. All 14 are located in the Front Range, either in the Indian Peaks Wilderness or Rocky Mountain National Park. These remnant glaciers survive at the highest elevations in east- to north-facing cirques near ridge crests—locations that are protected from the sun in summer and where snow accumulates in winter. Without these topographical features, it is unlikely the glaciers could survive. In fact, it is remarkable they are here at all. Colorado glaciers owe their existence to a rotor effect of wind that redistributes snow from both the west and the east slopes, depositing it in niches where the glaciers are found. They are referred to as wind-drift or Ural-type glaciers, named for the long north-south profile of the Front Range athwart prevailing westerly winds—a condition also found in the Ural Mountains of Russia.

At the close of the Little Ice Age, the earth's climate became warmer, and glaciers worldwide began to retreat. With the exception of a brief cooling period in the 1970s, temperatures have continued to climb. In fact, the planet warmed faster during the twentieth century than at any other time in the past thousand years. Since 1979 in particular, virtually all the world's glaciers have been retreating at unprecedented rates. This is certainly the case in the American West. If trends continue, Colorado's glaciers will be waning to extinction or near extinction by 2050.

To be sure, the planet is accustomed to cycles of warming and cooling. Within the past 750,000 years, a total of eight ice-age cycles have occurred, separated by warmer periods called interglacials. Going by this history, the earth is currently approaching the end of an interglacial, which means that another ice age is due in a few thousand years. Although it is not entirely clear what causes the cycles of glaciation, scientists believe it has something to do with astronomical rhythms. The earth's orbit around the sun is not uniform, varying between more circular and more elliptical paths. In addition, the tilt of the earth's axis increases and decreases over time as the planet spins, producing a wobble effect. These two factors together are believed to go a long way in determining the earth's glacial cycles, since they both affect the distribution of sunlight over the planet's surface.

Now it appears man is impacting these natural cycles. The burning of fossil fuels and clearing of forests have produced high levels of greenhouse gases in the atmosphere. Over the past 400,000 years, scientists have established a close correlation between periods of glaciation and levels of atmospheric CO_2. Lower CO_2 levels correspond with a cooler planet, while higher levels correspond with a warmer planet. Although it seems likely the current warming trend will continue into the near future, what is less clear is whether greenhouse warming will delay or perhaps even accelerate the coming of the next glacial. It also remains to be seen whether future changes in climate will be gradual or abrupt.

Bounding down the trail along the tumbling creek, on my way to the North and South glaciers, I think about the earth and what an extraordinary home it is—a tilted rock spinning in space, circling a star, with its own cycles of carbon and water to nurture the conditions of life over billions of years. Exquisite in its design and function. How lucky we are to be part of this complex interchange of atmosphere, ocean, and earth. This intricate dance of rock and fire, water and air.

The water we find today is essentially the same water that has existed on the planet for billions of years. The same substance, recycled through the ages in its own self-regulating system. Ice melts to become the water that becomes the cloud that becomes the rain that becomes the ice again. Water in its many places—glaciers, oceans, rivers, lakes, aquifers, clouds, the bodies of plants and animals and people. In its many processes—freezing, melting, evaporation, condensation, deposition, sublimation.

And the atmosphere—this thin layer of gases ten miles high, orchestrating a delicate balance between the capture and release of solar radiation. Between warming the planet and keeping it cool. This thin skin in the sky that modulates as the planet breathes. Like a living organism, Earth takes a deep breath every boreal spring and summer as the preponderance of its vegetation absorbs carbon dioxide from the air. Then, in autumn and winter when plants of the Northern Hemisphere decay, the planet exhales CO_2 back into the atmosphere.

What an extraordinary home, this earth. Full of momentous events of inhuman scale—asteroid hits, magnetic flips, supervolcanoes, ice ages, cataclysmic floods, earthquakes and hurricanes, tsunamis and tornadoes.

The planet will do what it will, with or without us. We'll learn to adapt, or not. In the final analysis, the question of whether man will survive on earth seems to be beside the point. Inconsequential. We mere mortals can only marvel at such magnificence and power, stand and watch in awe.

In space, this beautiful blue planet. This garden in the cosmos. This home. Paradise, indeed.

9. *The Way Home*

A sulphur butterfly darts beside the trail, its green eyespot winking in sun-light. On this spring day, Chautauqua Meadow shines with the yellows of cinquefoil and western wallflower, the purples of lupine and one-sided pen-stemon. A ponderosa releases a load of pollen to the wind. The sun slips be-hind a cloud. A magpie glides overhead.

I follow the trail to the top of the meadow where it forks above Bluebell Gulch. One way leads south to Royal Arch, the other west into the heart of the Flatirons—the five spires of fractured bedrock that rise a thousand feet above the valley floor. I take the way west and start up the steep gulch be-tween the second and third, climbing steadily for the ridge at the top where I'll sit a while on Sunset Rock, gazing across the foothills to the snowfields of the Divide shining in the afternoon sun. When I've had enough I'll drop over the saddle into the drainage that leads to Amphitheatre Rock, following the trail to the lower slopes of the meadow and eventually home. It's a hike I've made countless times, a circuitous route that seems fitting today given my in-clination to circle back on the years. It is nearly summer now, and my days at Chautauqua are winding down. Today, memory and imagination walk hand in hand. On the loose.

The trail leaves the meadow and enters a forest of ponderosa, mountain maple, spruce, and fir. I step across rocks and roots on my way past skunk-brush and sumac, kinnikinnick and Oregon grape. Along this steep trail the transitions in flora occur quickly. A plant community can be determined by any number of factors: soil type, moisture regime, microclimate, slope aspect, elevation, wind, erosion, fire, the habits of local wildlife. A small change in any of these can alter the species composition or phenology of a particular community. This spring, pasqueflower was virtually absent in lower elevations due to a late-season snow, while in higher elevations it bloomed readily only a short while later.

The penstemon blossoms seem bigger than what they were a few days ago. The quality of sunlight is sharper, too, thanks to a brisk westerly that pushes the haze east across the plains. A hummingbird whirs overhead, home now from its winter range along the equator. I could walk this route every afternoon for the rest of my days and never see the same place twice. All is in motion, tuned to the rhythms of daily and seasonal cycles.

Even the Flatirons, as implacable as they seem, reveal their different moods. At dawn they blush pink and rose with the first light of day. On other mornings they radiate a fiery orange, like molten rock turned inside out from the earth's core. During afternoon thunderstorms the towering pinnacles look somber under black clouds, as lightning flashes over Green Mountain and a cloudburst drains off the rock face along eroded grooves. In autumn, early snows darken the sandstone to deep chocolate beside a fringe of frosted pines. Autumn is also the season for western wildfires, and sometimes smoke from as far away as California hovers along the Front Range, casting an eerie pall over the outlying hills, turning the sunsets bloodred. In winter, ice fog obscures all but the highest crags that rise out of the ghostly shroud as if disengaged from solid earth. After big snows, long trails of spindrift blow off the high ridges like giant rooster tails in the wind.

The trail switchbacks up a sharp incline before splintering around large conifers, boulders, and deadfall. In this rugged terrain, it's difficult to keep a beaten path. At one point I follow a trail into the trees until it ends at the base of the second Flatiron. Hands against the rock, I look straight up the fifty-degree slope to the passing clouds above.

If the trail becomes lost at this point, I'm content to let the trees and boulders show me the way. And they do, but only if I keep a keen eye. Using the second and third as guides, I retrace my steps to the large ponderosa above the switchback that overlooks Kohler Mesa. In the trees below I look for the top of Tomato Rock—a spherical boulder some thirty feet in circumference that sits by itself among the ponderosas. How many times have I stood beside it, marveling at its singular shape and unlikely place among the trees? I often pass Tomato Rock on my way to the outcrop higher on the mesa, where a bed of pine needles fills a long depression in the stone. And how many times have I lain there, looking at the tops of ponderosas swaying in the wind, marking the subtle changes in the sky as day gave way to night? Not far from the mesa is the deep cave in the rugged gulch between the third and fourth. And close by it, Royal Arch. All are intimately familiar, all indelibly part of the place I call home.

It occurs to me as I walk that though my memories of this place are filtered now through the flux of emotion and desire, certain images and feelings still ring true. This is as authentic as memory claims, I suppose. Today, memory insists upon a pool of sunlight on the cabin floor in the stillness of afternoon. Picking dried flowers in November for a winter bouquet. Skiing the long slope by Gregory Canyon the morning after a snowstorm. Listening to a pack of coyotes under a March moon, yipping and howling in a warm chinook wind. Spending nights under a blanket in the ponderosas above Enchanted Mesa.

You'll have to pardon the nostalgia here, although I do think it's part of the overall picture. Just days ago I watched the faint figure of a man standing at the summit of the second Flatiron, his outline barely visible in a crown of brilliant light moments before the sun slipped behind the rock. Seventeen years ago I stood in the same place, peering down the rock face, beholding the full measure of mesas and plains below. And who was that person so many years ago? How do I begin to take stock of the man I once was? Of the paths taken and not taken, to arrive at this place *now*?

I continue up between the second and third, crossing a scree slope before entering the trees again and a maze of sandstone blocks. All the while, the Flatirons tower overhead—monuments of stone rising like gods in the sky. I come upon a boulder field and start across, choosing my steps carefully, admiring the intricate patterns of lichen that grow here in gray and gold and a shade of green not unlike the sheen of lime that covers the weathered third in spring. Or the green eyespot of the butterfly down in the meadow. Meanwhile, along the forest edge, penstemon blooms in the same shade of purple as the cloudy sky last evening that brought rain. Seeing the storm clouds hard against the lush green meadow, I couldn't help think of the same grasses in autumn, gold before a blue sky. Like the montage of Flatirons in different seasons and weather, I imagine the meadow and sky in all their various moods. A kaleidoscope of light and color in perpetual motion.

At the edge of the boulder field, a flowering bush stands like a sentinel before the forest. About four feet high with lovely white blossoms, the thimbleberry asserts its delicate beauty amid a bedlam of broken rock.

Into the trees again, I come upon a hidden oasis in the forest—a terraced garden of flowering plants surrounded by tall evergreens and enormous angled rock. Sunlight filters through the trees onto the grass and needle floor where a host of flowers and shrubs bloom: skunkbrush, yellow sulfur, primrose, penstemon, and cinquefoil. The flickering light plays upon sapling firs and ferns and the waxy leaves of lily of the valley. The petals of a wallflower bleed gold to orange to red. Meanwhile, a solitary cloud sails past the pinnacle of the third, pushed along by a steady west wind.

This is the miracle, it seems to me. All of it. Why any of this, when it seems just as likely there could be nothing at all? And it's here for everyone to see. But only if we drop all presumption of history, shed it like snakeskin. It's written that April is the cruelest month, and so it is. Cruel because its wealth of creative energy seems too overwhelming to bear, too sensuous and *alive* for principles and theorems to fathom. Cruel because it reminds us of our reluctance to embrace the chaotic beauty and wonder of the world. How can we ever divine the mystery of things without first capitulating to the bees and butterflies, the birds and blossoms?

Up the steep slope now and the last scramble to the ridge. Eyes of quartz set in stone watch as I go. Scrub pine grows stunted and twisted, well spaced. Testament to the wind and weather that scour this ridge.

Approaching the saddle, a panorama of foothills and snowy peaks unfolds. Along the back ridge I find Sunset Rock and climb to its top. Get myself situated. From here, the view looks north and west across plains and foothills and the high mountains of the Divide. To the north, a broad sweep of prairie grass rises to meet the first wave of foothills—a line of swells cresting in the familiar shapes of Sanitas, Flagstaff, Sugarloaf, and Lefthand. The foothills, in turn, rise to the lower snowfields and white-capped peaks shimmering in the west: Arapahoe, Niwot Ridge, Meeker, and Long's.

The analogy is not so far-fetched. After all, seventy million years ago, this was beach. The ancient sea that covered this area during the Cretaceous began to recede once the Front Range started its slow uplift. This local uplift raised the horizontal layers of sedimentary rock formed by the eroded deposits of the Ancestral Rockies. The sedimentary rock fractured and tilted into the striking formations we find today in such places as the Flatirons. Since then, the foothills and mountains have undergone their own process of erosion, resulting in a topography of canyons and valleys. The deposits of mud and gravel and sand, washed out of the canyons and carried onto the plains, form the mesas along the foothills.

In this perpetual cycle of upheaval and gradation, mountains rise only to be washed away by the forces of weathering and erosion. Rock changes to mud and sand and, in the case of the Flatirons, back to rock again. It's hard to think of the Flatirons in any other terms, hard to imagine them outside this circle of time. Like mountains, rocks exist in a continual state of transformation. Of the three major types of rock on earth—igneous, metamorphic, and sedimentary—all are subject to the processes that govern the rock cycle. All exist potentially in their other forms. In this cycle that knows no discernible beginning or end.

If we consider plate tectonics, we see that rock is moving in yet another way. According to the theory of continental drift, the earth's continents were connected in one or possibly two large landmasses as recently as two hundred million years ago. The supercontinent Pangaea broke apart sometime in the Mesozoic era, and the continents gradually drifted away from each other. As the North American continent drifted to the northwest during this time, much of the present United States was centered at about 30 degrees north latitude, providing warmer climates than what exist today.

On this walk up the mountain, I have come from grassland plains into a mixed montane forest. Looking west to the Divide from my seat on the rock, I see where the alpine forest gives way to a tundra ecosystem at timberline. Ever since the Tertiary period, the Rockies have been populated by an alpine tundra flora that exhibits close ties to the flora found in the mountains of central Asia, especially the Altai. Although the origins of this connection are not completely understood, other associations have been established between North American plants and the plants of other continents. For instance, a strong relationship exists between the flora of the Appalachian Mountains and the flora of Japan and China, both of which date back to the Tertiary. A similar relationship is seen in the flora of the Pacific Coast and eastern Asia. Some alpine areas in the Appalachians have a strong Amphi-Atlantic element. That is, they support species that are also found in the high mountains of Europe. Curiously, this element is practically nonexistent in the Rockies. Instead, the Rocky Mountain region shares a number of genera and even some species with the high mountains of Middle Asia. The Rocky Mountain flora seems to represent an alpine component of this ancient Tertiary flora of which the Appalachian and Pacific Coast floras constitute a lower-altitude, temperate one. One theory that could explain the Asian–Western American connection suggests that at one time a common Tertiary flora extended more or less continuously over a mountainous terrain that connected the two areas.

Continents drift, rock changes form. The planet spins on an axis on its way around the sun. "A world alive, always changing and moving," writes Leslie Marmon Silko, "and if you know where to look you can see it, sometimes almost imperceptible . . ."

I lay back against the boulder, palms flat against the rock. A few grains of sand come loose in my hand. Rubbing the granules between my fingers, I stare into the sky and feel the earth beneath me. The rock is *moving*. Minerals decomposing. Ions exchanging. A world of energy waves and particles in motion. All moving in a constant state of exchange and transformation. Form in transit, only energy remains. I imagine the various structural levels whirring, the hum of molecular vibration. The energy of rock.

The interchange knows no bounds. We too are open systems—subject to flows of energy, the cycling of matter, the transfer of information. It would be foolhardy to think of ourselves as somehow outside this process. In a very literal sense we are of the earth, its transitions and cycles. Richard Nelson writes: "There is nothing in me that is not of earth, no split instant of separateness, no particle that disunites me from the surroundings. . . . Like the cloud, I am transformed during every moment of my existence."

But how does one begin to find a place in this grand cosmic dance? How does one live in the face of such transience and impermanence?

Seventeen years ago, I stood at the top of the second Flatiron and gazed across the plains. Looking back now, I see a younger self—driven by expectation and the prospects of a wide-open future. What I remember most about those early years was simply the desire to get out and see new places. At first, it seemed enough just to be *out there* in some of the more remote backcountry of the mountain West—either alone or, as was usually the case, with a friend or two. Over time, I recognized there was something about these experiences I needed—the exploration and discovery, the challenge, the quest. Moreover, inasmuch as nothing we were doing was unique or original or required any special expertise, and that we felt compelled to repeat the experiences again and again, it occurred to me that we were engaged in some kind of loose ritual. Finding a rhythm along the contours of a mountain, keeping trim with the current...all of this put us in a special *relation* with the world. The aesthetic perception of these experiences presented us with a way of life. It was the best way we knew to make contact. To make a meaningful connection with the world.

Ultimately, of course, I began to consider these experiences as opportunities for storytelling. In the process of reflecting on them, I began to weave a story that I could understand and live by. Explorations of geography became explorations of self. Adventures led to meditations, which led to speculation, which in turn led to some kind of mythopoesis. As much as the experiences helped locate us in the world, their stories gave us a way to comprehend it.

The wind has died down. The sun has fallen behind a bank of clouds hovering over the Divide. A full moon rises over the eastern horizon to begin its luminous arc across the night sky.

We tramp a perpetual journey, Whitman wrote. And so it is.

I get up to leave, brushing the sand from my jeans. From the rock I can see where the trail drops sharply over the saddle, switchbacking down into the gulch. This is my path, I think. The way home.